THE DASH DIET COOKBOOK FOR BEGINNERS

By

Jane F Garraway

Copyright © 2024

TABLE OF CONTENT

SCAN HERE TO CHECK OUT OTHER BOOKS BY JANE GARRAWAY

Welcome!

I am thrilled to have you purchase this cookbook. Whether you are an experienced home cook or just starting out, my collection of recipes is always designed to inspire and my goal is to make cooking an enjoyable and healthy experience for everyone.

Within these pages, you'll find a diverse range of dishes, each crafted with love and attention to detail.

Cooking is not just about preparing food; it's about creating memories, exploring new flavors, and sharing delicious and healthy meals with your loved ones. I encourage you to experiment, make these recipes your own, and savor every moment of the process.

Thank you for allowing me to be a part of your journey. Let's get cooking!

Jane Garraway

GETTING STARTED: DASH DIET 101

The **DASH** diet, is a well-regarded eating plan that promotes a balanced and healthy lifestyle. It was developed by the National Heart, Lung, and Blood Institute (NHLBI), a part of the U.S. National Institutes of Health.

The DASH diet was initially created to help individuals manage high blood pressure, but its benefits extend beyond. The NHLBI sponsored several research studies to determine the most effective way of reducing blood pressure through dietary changes. By combining key nutrients in specific proportions, the DASH diet emerged as an effective solution.

The acronym DASH stands for "**D**ietary **A**pproaches to **S**top **H**ypertension." Its main objective is to lower blood pressure and prevent hypertension, which is a common risk factor for heart disease and stroke. However, the DASH diet is not solely focused on hypertension; it can also promote overall health and well-being.

Recognized by:
The DASH diet has received approval and endorsement from various health organizations worldwide. Some prominent bodies that recommend the DASH diet include:

National Heart, Lung, and Blood Institute (NHLBI)
The NHLBI developed and continues to promote the DASH diet as an evidence-based approach to reduce blood pressure.

American Heart Association (AHA)
The AHA recognizes the DASH diet as an effective way to manage blood pressure and improve cardiovascular health.

Dietary Guidelines for Americans
The DASH diet is recommended by the U.S. Department of Agriculture (USDA) and the U.S. Department of Health and Human Services (HHS) as part of their dietary guidelines.

World Health Organization (WHO)
The WHO highlights the DASH diet as a healthy eating plan that can contribute to the prevention and control of noncommunicable diseases, including hypertension.
This recognition highlight the effectiveness and well-founded nature of the DASH diet as a sensible and nutritious approach to improving overall health, managing blood pressure, and reducing the risk of cardiovascular diseases. →

Key Characteristics And Benefits Of The Dash Diet:

- Emphasizes nutrient-rich foods: The DASH diet encourages consuming foods that are rich in essential nutrients like fruits, vegetables, whole grains, lean proteins, and low-fat dairy products. These foods provide a wide range of vitamins, minerals, and antioxidants that support overall health.

- Low in sodium: The DASH diet limits sodium intake, making it beneficial for those with high blood pressure. By reducing sodium, it helps to lower blood pressure levels, thus decreasing the risk of heart disease and stroke.

- **Focuses on whole grains:** Whole grains like brown rice, whole wheat bread, and oats are a staple in the DASH diet. They are high in fiber and help maintain a feeling of fullness, regulate blood sugar levels, and support digestive health.

- **Includes a variety of fruits and vegetables:** The DASH diet promotes consuming a diverse range of colorful fruits and vegetables. These are excellent sources of vitamins, minerals, and fiber, and have been associated with a lower risk of chronic diseases, including heart disease and certain types of cancer.

- **Encourages lean protein sources:** The DASH diet suggests incorporating lean protein sources like poultry, fish, beans, and nuts. These protein options are lower in saturated fat and can contribute to maintaining muscle mass and promoting satiety.

- **Limits sugary and processed foods:** The DASH diet advises reducing foods high in added sugars, saturated fats, and processed ingredients. By minimizing these unhealthy options like sugary beverages, pastries, and processed snacks, the diet helps improve overall nutrition and reduce the risk of chronic diseases.

Benefits Of The Dash Diet Include:

→**Lowering high blood pressure:** The DASH diet is proven to effectively reduce blood pressure levels, helping manage hypertension and decrease the risk of heart disease and stroke.

→**Supporting heart health:** By focusing on nutrient-rich foods and reducing sodium intake, the DASH diet can improve overall heart health and reduce the risk of cardiovascular diseases.

→**Promoting overall well-being:** The DASH diet encourages a balanced and varied eating plan that provides all the necessary nutrients for optimal health. Its emphasis on fruits, vegetables, whole grains, and lean proteins contributes to maintaining a healthy weight, boosting energy levels, and supporting overall well-being.

→**Collaborating with other healthy habits:** The DASH diet complements other healthy lifestyle practices such as regular physical activity and avoiding tobacco and excessive alcohol consumption. These combined efforts can enhance the benefits and promote a healthier lifestyle.

The DASH diet's characteristics and benefits make it a sensible choice for those aiming to improve their overall health, manage blood pressure, and reduce the risk of chronic diseases, while still enjoying a wide range of nutritious and flavorful foods.

Key Components Of The Dash Diet

→**Fruits and Vegetables:**
The DASH diet encourages a high intake of fruits and vegetables. These foods are rich in vitamins, minerals, antioxidants, and fiber, all of which contribute to heart health and overall well-being. Aim to include a variety of colorful fruits and vegetables in your diet.

→**Whole Grains:**
Whole grains like brown rice, whole wheat, oats, quinoa, and whole grain bread are emphasized in the DASH diet. They provide complex carbohydrates and dietary fiber, which can help regulate blood sugar levels and promote fullness.

→Lean Proteins:
The DASH diet suggests incorporating lean sources of protein, such as skinless poultry, fish, lean cuts of meat, eggs, legumes (beans and lentils), and tofu. These options are lower in saturated fats and can help maintain muscle mass and keep you satisfied.

→Low-Fat Dairy:
Low-fat or fat-free dairy products, such as milk, yogurt, and cheese, are included in the DASH diet. They provide essential nutrients like calcium and vitamin D while reducing saturated fat intake.

→Nuts, Seeds, and Legumes:
Nuts and seeds, including almonds, walnuts, flaxseeds, and chia seeds, are recommended in moderation due to their heart-healthy fats and nutrient content. Legumes like beans and lentils are excellent sources of plant-based protein and fiber.

→Healthy Fats:
The DASH diet encourages the consumption of healthy fats found in foods like avocados, nuts, seeds, and olive oil. These fats can help improve cholesterol levels and provide energy.

→Limited Sodium:
One of the primary goals of the DASH diet is to reduce sodium intake. Excessive sodium consumption can contribute to high blood pressure. The diet recommends limiting salt intake and choosing foods that are lower in sodium.

→Limiting Added Sugars:
While the DASH diet doesn't eliminate carbohydrates entirely, it advises against consuming foods and beverages high in added sugars. This approach can help manage blood sugar levels and reduce the risk of cardiovascular issues.

→Moderation and Portion Control:
The DASH diet emphasizes moderation in all food groups and portion control. This helps prevent overeating and ensures a balanced intake of nutrients.

→Balanced Approach:
The DASH diet is not extreme or restrictive. It emphasizes a balanced intake of various nutrients, encouraging a variety of foods from different food groups to meet your nutritional needs.

→Physical Activity:
While not a food component, regular physical activity is an important part of the DASH diet. Combining a healthy diet with exercise can contribute to overall cardiovascular health.

The DASH diet's focus on nutrient-rich foods, low sodium intake, and moderation aligns well with general guidelines for promoting heart health and overall well-being. It's important to consult with a healthcare professional or registered dietitian before starting any new diet, especially if you have specific health concerns or dietary needs.

THE DASH DIET FOOD GROUPS

The DASH diet emphasizes a balanced intake of various food groups to promote good health and manage blood pressure. Here is a comprehensive overview of the food groups and a sample food list based on the DASH diet:

→**Vegetables:**
Aim for 4-5 servings of vegetables every day.
Include a variety of colorful options like spinach, broccoli, carrots, peppers, sweet potatoes, and tomatoes. They can be enjoyed raw, steamed, roasted, or in soups and salads.

→**Fruits:**
Consume 4-5 servings of fruits daily.
Opt for fresh, frozen, or canned fruits without added sugars. Some great choices include berries, apples, oranges, bananas, grapes, and melons. Enjoy them as snacks, in smoothies, or as part of a fruit salad.

→**Grains:**
Include 6-8 servings of grains each day, with a focus on whole grains.
Incorporate whole wheat bread, brown rice, oatmeal, quinoa, whole wheat pasta, and whole grain cereals. These provide fiber, vitamins, and minerals. Choose options without added sugars or excessive sodium.

→**Lean proteins:**
Aim for 6 or fewer servings of lean protein sources daily.
Include skinless poultry, fish (such as salmon, tuna, or cod), legumes (such as beans, lentils, or chickpeas), tofu, and unsalted nuts and seeds. These are good sources of protein, vitamins, and minerals while being lower in saturated fat compared to other protein sources.

→**Dairy:**
Include 2-3 servings of low-fat dairy products each day, such as skimmed milk, low-fat yogurt, or reduced-fat cheese. These provide calcium and other essential nutrients.
If lactose-intolerant, opt for lactose-free or fortified plant-based alternatives like almond milk or soy yogurt.

→ **Fats and oils:**
Focus on healthy fats in moderation, while limiting saturated and trans fats.
Choose sources like olive oil, canola oil, avocados, and nuts. Avoid or reduce the intake of foods high in unhealthy fats like fried foods, butter, and full-fat dairy products.

→**Nuts, seeds, and legumes:**
These are sources of healthy fats, protein, and fiber.
Include options like almonds, peanuts, walnuts, flaxseeds, chia seeds, lentils, and black beans in your meals and snacks. To visualize the recommended servings for each food group, the DASH diet pyramid can be helpful:
1. The base of the pyramid consists of grains and grain products, recommending 6-8 servings per day.
2. The next level emphasizes vegetables and fruits, suggesting 4-5 servings of each daily.
3. Following that, include 2-3 servings of low-fat dairy products and 6 or fewer daily servings of lean proteins.
4. At the top of the pyramid, you find fats, oils, and sweets, which should be consumed sparingly.

To make it easier to follow the DASH diet, here is a sample food list:
→ **Grains**: Whole-wheat bread, brown rice, quinoa, oatmeal, whole-grain pasta
→ **Vegetables**: Leafy greens, carrots, broccoli, sweet potatoes, tomatoes, cucumbers
→ **Fruits**: Apples, bananas, berries, oranges, grapes, pineapple
→ **Dairy**: Low-fat or fat-free milk, yogurt, cheese
→ **Protein**: Chicken, fish, beans, tofu, lean beef
→ **Fats and oils:** Olive oil, avocado, nuts, seeds

Remember that these are general guidelines, and individual needs may vary. When following the DASH diet, it is important to consider portion sizes, limit sodium intake, and maintain an overall balanced and varied eating plan.

DASH Diet Food List

Below is an extended list of foods allowed and not allowed in each category of the DASH diet:

Fruits
Allowed:
- Berries (blueberries, strawberries, raspberries)
- Apples
- Oranges
- Bananas
- Grapes
- Peaches
- Pears
- Kiwi
- Melons (watermelon, cantaloupe)
- Citrus fruits (grapefruits, mandarins)
- Pineapple

Not Allowed:
- Fruits with added sugars
- Fruit juices high in added sugars

Vegetables
Allowed:
- Leafy greens (spinach, kale, collard greens)
- Broccoli
- Carrots
- Bell peppers
- Tomatoes
- Cucumbers
- Cauliflower
- Brussels sprouts
- Zucchini
- Onions
- Sweet potatoes

Not Allowed:
- Vegetables cooked with excessive salt or butter

Grains

Allowed:
- Whole wheat bread
- Brown rice
- Quinoa
- Oats
- Barley
- Whole grain pasta
- Whole grain cereal
- Whole grain crackers

Not Allowed:
- White bread
- White rice
- Highly processed cereals

Lean Proteins
Allowed:
- Skinless poultry (chicken, turkey)
- Fish (salmon, mackerel, tuna)
- Lean cuts of beef or pork
- Eggs
- Legumes (beans, lentils, peas)
- Tofu
- Nuts and seeds (in moderation)

Not Allowed:
- Fatty cuts of meat
- Processed meats (sausages, bacon)
- Fried proteins

Dairy
Allowed:
- Low-fat or fat-free milk
- Low-fat or fat-free yogurt
- Low-fat or fat-free cheese
- Dairy alternatives (soy milk, almond milk, etc.)

Not Allowed:
- Full-fat dairy products
- Dairy products high in added sugars

Nuts, Seeds, and Legumes
Allowed:
- Almonds
- Walnuts
- Flaxseeds
- Chia seeds
- Peanuts (in moderation)
- Lentils
- Chickpeas
- Black beans
- Kidney beans

Not Allowed:
- Nuts and seeds with added salt or sugar

Fats and Oils
Allowed:
- Olive oil
- Canola oil
- Avocado
- Nuts and seeds (in moderation)

Not Allowed:
- Trans fats
- Excessively fatty or fried foods

Sweets
Allowed:
- Occasional small portions of dark chocolate
- Fresh fruit-based desserts

Not Allowed:
- Sweets high in added sugars
- Pastries and heavily processed desserts

Remember, portion control and moderation are key components of the DASH diet. Also, it's important to consult with a healthcare professional or registered dietitian before making significant dietary changes, especially if you have any underlying health conditions.

PART ONE

SMOOTHIES

Avocado Smoothie

This creamy and refreshing avocado smoothie is a perfect breakfast or snack option that fits perfectly with the DASH diet. It's packed with healthy fats, potassium, and fiber from the avocado, while keeping sodium and added sugar in check.

 **Prep Time:** 5 minutes || **Cook Time:** N/A || **Yield:** 1 serving

INGREDIENTS
- ½ ripe avocado
- 1 cup unsweetened almond milk (or low-fat dairy milk)
- ½ cup frozen spinach
- 1 banana, frozen or fresh
- ½ tablespoon lemon juice
- ¼ teaspoon ground cinnamon
- Pinch of ground ginger (optional)
- Handful of ice cubes (optional)

INSTRUCTIONS
1. If using fresh banana, chop it into chunks and freeze for at least 30 minutes before blending.
2. Add all ingredients – avocado, almond milk, spinach, banana, lemon juice, cinnamon, ginger (if using), and ice cubes (if using) – to a blender.
3. Blend until smooth and creamy. You may need to add more liquid or scrape down the sides occasionally for even blending.
4. Pour the smoothie into a glass and enjoy!

NOTES
- Choose a ripe but firm avocado for the smoothie. It will blend easier and have a creamier texture.
- Frozen spinach adds a nutritional boost without overpowering the taste. You can also use kale for a slightly different flavor profile.
- If the smoothie is too thick, add a little more almond milk or water, one tablespoon at a time, until it reaches your desired consistency.
- For a sweeter smoothie, add a few drops of stevia or a sprinkle of monk fruit sweetener.
- You can experiment with different fruits and vegetables suitable for the DASH diet. Frozen berries, mango, or chopped cucumber can be added for a variety of flavors.
- For an extra protein boost, add a scoop of unflavored protein powder to the smoothie.

NUTRITIONAL INFORMATION (approximate per serving):
Calories: 300 | Protein: 4g | Fat: 15g | Carbohydrates: 30g | Sodium: 50mg (depending on sodium content of ingredients) | Potassium: 600mg (depending on ingredients)

Strawberry-Banana-Blueberry Smoothie

This refreshing and vibrant smoothie is a perfect example of a delicious and nutritious drink option for the DASH diet. Packed with heart-healthy fruits and low in sodium, it's a great way to start your day or enjoy a satisfying snack.

 **Prep Time:** 5 minutes || **Cook Time:** N/A || **Yield:** 1 serving

INGREDIENTS
- ½ cup frozen strawberries
- ½ cup frozen blueberries
- ½ ripe banana, frozen or fresh
- 1 cup unsweetened almond milk (or low-fat dairy milk)
- ½ cup plain low-fat Greek yogurt (optional, for added protein)
- ¼ cup chopped fresh spinach (optional, for an extra nutrient boost)
- Squeeze of lemon juice (optional)
- Handful of ice cubes (optional)

INSTRUCTIONS
1. If using fresh banana, chop it into chunks and freeze for at least 30 minutes before blending.
2. Add all ingredients – frozen strawberries, frozen blueberries, banana, almond milk, Greek yogurt (if using), spinach (if using), lemon juice (if using), and ice cubes (if using) – to a blender.
3. Blend until smooth and creamy. You may need to add more liquid or scrape down the sides occasionally for even blending.
4. Pour the smoothie into a glass and enjoy!

NOTES
- Use frozen fruit for a thicker and frostier smoothie.
- You can adjust the amount of fruit to your preference. For a sweeter smoothie, add more banana or a sprinkle of stevia or monk fruit sweetener.
- If the smoothie is too thick, add a little more almond milk or water, one tablespoon at a time, until it reaches your desired consistency.
- For a protein boost and creamier texture, add the Greek yogurt.
- Spinach adds a nutritional boost without overpowering the taste. You can also use kale for a slightly different flavor profile.
- This smoothie is a great base for customization. You can experiment with other DASH-friendly fruits like mango, peaches, or pineapple.

Adding Yogurt and Spinach:
- Including the ½ cup of plain low-fat Greek yogurt will increase the protein content to around 6g per serving.
- Adding the ¼ cup of chopped fresh spinach will add minimal sodium and boost the potassium content slightly.

NUTRITIONAL INFORMATION (approximate per serving, without yogurt and spinach):
Calories: 200 | Protein: 1g | Fat: 2g | Carbohydrates: 35g | Sodium: 50mg (depending on sodium content of ingredients) | Potassium: 400mg (depending on ingredients)

Banana Almond Smoothie

This creamy and satisfying banana almond smoothie is a perfect on-the-go breakfast or afternoon snack option for the DASH diet. Packed with potassium from the banana, protein and healthy fats from the almond butter and milk, and a touch of cinnamon for warmth, it delivers a delicious and nutritious drink that keeps sodium in check.

 **Prep Time:** 5 minutes || **Cook Time:** No cook || **Yield:** 1 serving

INGREDIENTS
- 1 ripe banana, frozen (preferred) or fresh
- 1 cup unsweetened almond milk (or low-fat dairy milk)
- 1 tablespoon almond butter (unsweetened)
- ½ cup plain, low-fat Greek yogurt (optional, for added protein and creaminess)
- ½ teaspoon ground cinnamon
- Pinch of ground nutmeg (optional)
- Few ice cubes (optional, depending on desired consistency)

INSTRUCTIONS
1. Place all ingredients (banana, almond milk, almond butter, Greek yogurt if using, cinnamon, nutmeg if using, and ice cubes if using) into a blender. Blend until smooth and creamy.
2. Pour the banana almond smoothie into a glass and enjoy it immediately.

NOTES
- **Frozen banana:** Using a frozen banana creates a thicker and creamier smoothie texture without the need for additional ice cubes.
- **Milk options:** Unsweetened almond milk is a DASH-friendly option, but low-fat dairy milk can be used as well.
- **Almond butter selection:** Choose unsweetened almond butter with no added sugar or salt for a lower-sodium option.
- **Greek yogurt:** Adding plain, low-fat Greek yogurt boosts protein content and adds creaminess, but it's not essential. Opt for unsweetened varieties.
- **Sweetener options:** This recipe is naturally sweetened by the banana. If desired, add a touch of honey or maple syrup for additional sweetness, but use them sparingly.
- **Leftovers:** Smoothies are best enjoyed fresh, but leftover smoothie can be stored in an airtight container in the refrigerator for up to 24 hours. The texture might become thicker due to separation, so stir well before re-consuming.

NUTRITIONAL INFORMATION (approximate per serving):
Calories: 250 | Protein: 10g (with Greek yogurt) | Fat: 10g | Carbohydrates: 30g | Sodium: 150mg (depending on sodium content of ingredients) | Potassium: 450mg (depending on ingredients)

Green Glow Smoothie

This refreshing and flavorful green smoothie is a perfect on-the-go breakfast or snack option that adheres to the DASH diet. Packed with vitamins, minerals, and antioxidants from the greens and fruits, this recipe keeps sodium content low and uses natural sweetness for a delicious and healthy drink.

 **Prep Time:** 5 minutes || **Yield:** 1 serving

INGREDIENTS
- 1 cup unsweetened almond milk (or low-fat milk)
- ½ cup frozen spinach
- ½ banana, frozen (ripe)
- ¼ cup chopped cucumber (optional)
- 1 tablespoon chopped fresh mint or parsley
- ¼ teaspoon ground ginger

INSTRUCTIONS
1. In a blender, combine the unsweetened almond milk (or low-fat milk), frozen spinach, frozen banana, chopped cucumber (optional), chopped fresh mint or parsley, and ground ginger.
2. Blend on high speed until the mixture is smooth and creamy, scraping down the sides as needed.
3. Pour the smoothie into a glass and enjoy immediately!

NOTES
- Using frozen spinach and banana creates a thicker and frostier smoothie texture. You can use fresh spinach and a few ice cubes if preferred.
- Unsweetened almond milk or low-fat milk can be used. Opt for unsweetened varieties to control added sugars.
- Chopped cucumber adds a refreshing element to the smoothie, but you can omit it if desired.
- You can experiment with different greens like kale or romaine lettuce. For a sweeter taste, add a few berries like blueberries or raspberries.

NUTRITIONAL INFORMATION (approximate per serving):
Calories: 200 | Protein: 5g | Fat: 5g | Carbohydrates: 30g | Sodium: 30mg (depending on sodium content of ingredients) | Potassium: 500mg (depending on ingredients)

Mango Ginger Smoothie

This refreshing and flavorful smoothie is a perfect fit for the DASH diet. Packed with vitamin C and antioxidants from the mango and ginger, this recipe keeps sodium in check by using low-sodium ingredients and natural sweetness from the fruit.

 **Prep Time:** 5 minutes || **Yield:** 1 serving

INGREDIENTS
- 1 cup frozen mango chunks
- ½ cup unsweetened almond milk (or low-fat milk)
- ½ cup plain, non-fat Greek yogurt
- 1 teaspoon chopped fresh ginger
- ¼ teaspoon ground cinnamon (optional)
- Pinch of ground cardamom (optional)

INSTRUCTIONS
1. In a blender, combine the frozen mango chunks, unsweetened almond milk (or low-fat milk), plain, non-fat Greek yogurt, chopped fresh ginger, ground cinnamon (optional), and ground cardamom (optional).
2. Blend on high speed until the mixture is smooth and creamy, scraping down the sides as needed.
3. Pour the smoothie into a glass and enjoy immediately!

NOTES
- **Frozen mango:** Frozen mango chunks are convenient and add a thick and frosty texture to the smoothie. You can substitute fresh mango if preferred, but you may need to add a little ice for a thicker consistency.
- **Milk options:** Unsweetened almond milk or low-fat milk can be used. Opt for unsweetened varieties to control added sugars.
- **Ginger variation:** You can adjust the amount of ginger to your preference. Start with a smaller amount and add more to taste if desired.
- **Toppings (optional):** For an extra touch of flavor and texture, top your smoothie with a sprinkle of chopped fresh mint or a dollop of low-fat whipped cream.

NUTRITIONAL INFORMATION (approximate per serving):
Calories: 250 | Protein: 15g | Fat: 5g | Carbohydrates: 35g | Sodium: 80mg (depending on sodium content of ingredients) | Potassium: 500mg (depending on ingredients)

PART TWO

BREAKFAST

Low-Sodium Waffles

These fluffy and flavorful waffles are perfect for a heart-healthy breakfast on the DASH diet. Made with whole-wheat flour and low-sodium ingredients, they deliver deliciousness without compromising your dietary goals.

 **Prep Time:** 10 minutes || **Cook Time:** 10 minutes per waffle || **Yield:** 4-6 waffles (depending on waffle iron size)

INGREDIENTS
- 1 ¾ cups whole-wheat flour
- 2 teaspoons baking powder
- 1 teaspoon ground cinnamon
- ¼ teaspoon ground nutmeg (optional)
- 2 tablespoons granulated sugar substitute (such as stevia or erythritol)
- 1 ½ cups unsweetened almond milk (or low-sodium dairy milk)
- 2 large eggs
- 2 tablespoons melted unsalted butter, cooled slightly
- 1 teaspoon vanilla extract

INSTRUCTIONS
1. Preheat your waffle iron. In a large bowl, whisk together the whole-wheat flour, baking powder, cinnamon, nutmeg (if using), and sugar substitute.
2. In a separate bowl, whisk together the almond milk, eggs, melted butter, and vanilla extract.
3. Pour the wet ingredients into the dry ingredients and whisk gently until just combined. Do not overmix, a few lumps are okay.
4. Lightly spray your waffle iron with non-stick cooking spray. Pour batter into the waffle iron, typically using about ½ cup of batter per waffle.
5. Close the lid and cook for 3-5 minutes, or until golden brown and cooked through. Steam will begin to release from the sides when the waffle is done.
6. Carefully remove the waffle from the iron and place on a wire rack to keep warm. Repeat with remaining batter.

NOTES
- For a vegan option, use a flaxseed egg instead of regular eggs. Mix 1 tablespoon of ground flaxseed with 3 tablespoons of water, let sit for 5 minutes until thickened, then use in place of one egg.
- You can substitute whole-wheat pastry flour for a slightly lighter texture.
- If your waffle iron doesn't have a non-stick coating, you can brush it with a thin layer of melted butter before adding the batter.
- You can experiment with different toppings suitable for the DASH diet. Try sliced fruit with a drizzle of low-fat maple syrup, chopped nuts, or a dollop of low-fat yogurt.

NUTRITIONAL INFORMATION (approximate per waffle):
Calories: 250 | Protein: 8g | Fat: 10g | Carbohydrates: 35g | Sodium: 200mg (depending on sodium content of ingredients) | Potassium: 150mg (depending on ingredients)

Banana Chia Overnight Oats

This delicious and nutritious overnight oats recipe is a perfect grab-and-go breakfast option for the DASH diet. It's packed with fiber and protein from the chia seeds and oats, and naturally low in sodium. The banana adds sweetness without added sugar.

 **Prep Time:** 5 minutes || **Cook Time:** N/A || **Yield:** 1 serving

INGREDIENTS
- ½ cup rolled oats
- ½ cup unsweetened almond milk (or low-fat dairy milk)
- ½ banana, mashed
- 1 tablespoon chia seeds
- ¼ teaspoon ground cinnamon
- Pinch of salt
- Toppings (optional):
  - Sliced banana
  - Chopped nuts (almonds, walnuts, pecans)
  - Berries (strawberries, blueberries, raspberries)
  - A sprinkle of grated low-fat mozzarella cheese (optional)

INSTRUCTIONS
1. In a small jar or container, combine the rolled oats, almond milk, mashed banana, chia seeds, cinnamon, and salt. Stir well to combine all ingredients.
2. Cover the jar tightly with a lid or plastic wrap. Refrigerate for at least 4 hours, or overnight for best results.
3. In the morning, take out the oats from the fridge. The chia seeds will have absorbed the liquid and the oats will be softened.
4. Stir the oats before adding your desired toppings.

NOTES
- Use rolled oats instead of quick oats for a chewier texture.
- You can use other types of milk such as oat milk, soy milk, or coconut milk (unsweetened) depending on your preference.
- For a creamier texture, add 1-2 tablespoons of low-fat plain Greek yogurt to the overnight oats mixture.
- To make this recipe ahead of time, you can prepare multiple jars for the week and store them in the refrigerator for up to 3 days.
- Get creative with your toppings! Chopped apple, dried fruit (raisins, cranberries), or a drizzle of low-fat honey are all DASH-friendly options.
- While mozzarella cheese is a source of calcium, it's higher in sodium. Use it sparingly or omit it completely to strictly adhere to the DASH diet.

NUTRITIONAL INFORMATION (approximate per serving):
Calories: 250 | Protein: 5g | Fat: 5g | Carbohydrates: 40g | Sodium: 60mg (depending on sodium content of ingredients) | Potassium: 200mg (depending on ingredients)

Banana Oatmeal Pancakes

These fluffy and satisfying banana oatmeal pancakes are a perfect breakfast option for the DASH diet. Packed with fiber from the oats and potassium from the banana, they are naturally lower in sodium and keep you feeling full for longer.

Prep Time: 10 minutes || **Cook Time:** 15-20 minutes || **Yield:** 4-5 pancakes

INGREDIENTS
- ½ cup rolled oats (not quick oats)
- ½ cup whole wheat flour
- 1 teaspoon baking powder
- ½ teaspoon ground cinnamon
- ¼ teaspoon ground nutmeg (optional)
- Pinch of salt
- 1 ripe banana, mashed
- ¾ cup unsweetened almond milk (or low-fat dairy milk)
- 1 egg
- 1 tablespoon canola oil

INSTRUCTIONS
1. In a medium bowl, whisk together the dry ingredients: rolled oats, whole wheat flour, baking powder, cinnamon, nutmeg (if using), and salt.
2. In a separate bowl, mash the ripe banana. Add the almond milk (or dairy milk), egg, and canola oil to the mashed banana and whisk until well combined.
3. Pour the wet ingredients into the dry ingredients and stir until just combined. Be careful not to overmix, as this can lead to tough pancakes. There may be a few small lumps, which is fine.
4. Heat a lightly greased non-stick pan or griddle over medium heat. For each pancake, pour about ¼ cup of batter onto the pan.
5. Cook the pancakes for 2-3 minutes per side, or until golden brown and bubbles appear on the surface. Flip the pancakes carefully and cook for an additional 1-2 minutes, or until cooked through.
6. Serve the pancakes warm with your favorite toppings.

NOTES
- Use a ripe banana for the best sweetness and flavor.
- If the batter seems too thick, add a tablespoon or two of additional almond milk (or dairy milk) until it reaches a pourable consistency.
- For a vegan option, use a flaxseed egg instead of a regular egg. To make a flaxseed egg, combine 1 tablespoon of ground flaxseed with 3 tablespoons of water and let it sit for 5 minutes before using.
- You can experiment with different DASH-friendly toppings. Here are some ideas:
  - Sliced banana with a sprinkle of cinnamon
  - Berries (strawberries, blueberries, raspberries)
  - Chopped nuts (almonds, walnuts, pecans)
  - A dollop of low-fat plain Greek yogurt with a drizzle of honey
  - Low-sodium maple syrup

NUTRITIONAL INFORMATION (approximate per serving):
Calories: 250 | Protein: 6g | Fat: 8g | Carbohydrates: 35g | Sodium: 150mg (depending on sodium content of ingredients) | Potassium: 400mg (depending on ingredients)

Mediterranean Egg Bites

These protein-packed and flavorful egg bites are a perfect meal prep option for the DASH diet. Filled with Mediterranean ingredients like sun-dried tomatoes, spinach, and feta cheese, they are naturally lower in sodium and keep you feeling satisfied on the go.

 **Prep Time:** 10 minutes || **Cook Time:** 15-20 minutes || **Yield:** 12 egg bites

INGREDIENTS
- 6 eggs, beaten
- ½ cup chopped fresh spinach
- ¼ cup chopped sun-dried tomatoes (not packed in oil)
- ¼ cup crumbled feta cheese
- ¼ cup chopped red onion
- 1 tablespoon chopped fresh parsley
- ¼ teaspoon dried oregano
- Pinch of salt and freshly ground black pepper

INSTRUCTIONS
1. Preheat oven to 375°F (190°C). Lightly grease a muffin tin or spray with non-stick cooking spray.
2. In a large bowl, whisk together the beaten eggs, chopped spinach, sun-dried tomatoes, feta cheese, red onion, parsley, oregano, salt, and pepper.
3. Divide the egg mixture evenly among the prepared muffin tin cups.
4. Bake for 15-20 minutes, or until the egg bites are set and cooked through. You can insert a toothpick into the center of an egg bite and if it comes out clean, they are done.
5. Let the egg bites cool slightly before removing them from the muffin tin. They can be served warm or at room temperature.

NOTES
- If you don't have fresh spinach, you can use 1 cup of frozen chopped spinach, thawed and squeezed dry.
- For a vegetarian option, omit the feta cheese and add an extra ¼ cup of chopped vegetables like bell peppers or mushrooms.
- You can also add a teaspoon of chopped fresh dill or crumbled cooked chicken breast to the egg mixture for additional flavor and protein.
- Leftover egg bites can be stored in an airtight container in the refrigerator for up to 3 days. Reheat gently in the microwave or oven before serving.

NUTRITIONAL INFORMATION (approximate per serving):
Calories: 120 | Protein: 7g | Fat: 6g | Carbohydrates: 3g | Sodium: 200mg (depending on sodium content of ingredients) | Potassium: 150mg (depending on ingredients)

Cinnamon Apple Breakfast Rice

This warm and comforting dish is a perfect twist on oatmeal for the DASH diet. Packed with fiber-rich brown rice, protein from nuts, and naturally sweet apples, it's a delicious and satisfying breakfast option that keeps sodium in check.

Prep Time: 10 minutes || **Cook Time:** 30-35 minutes || **Yield:** 2 servings

INGREDIENTS
- ½ cup brown rice, rinsed
- 1 cup unsweetened almond milk (or low-fat dairy milk)
- 1 cup water
- ½ teaspoon ground cinnamon
- Pinch of salt
- 1 medium apple, diced (tart or sweet variety)
- ¼ cup chopped walnuts or pecans
- 1 tablespoon raisins (optional)
- 1 tablespoon chopped fresh parsley (optional)

INSTRUCTIONS
1. In a medium saucepan, combine the rinsed brown rice, almond milk (or dairy milk), water, cinnamon, and salt. Bring to a boil over medium heat.
2. Reduce heat, cover the pan, and simmer for 30-35 minutes, or until the rice is cooked through and the liquid is absorbed.
3. While the rice is cooking, prepare the apples. Dice the apple into bite-sized pieces.
4. In the last 5 minutes of cooking, add the diced apples to the rice pot. Stir gently to combine.
5. Once the rice is cooked and the apples are softened, remove the pan from heat.
6. Fluff the rice with a fork and stir in the chopped nuts and raisins (if using).
7. Serve the cinnamon apple breakfast rice warm in bowls. Garnish with a sprinkle of chopped fresh parsley (optional).

NOTES
- You can use pre-cooked brown rice to save time on prepping. However, using cooked rice might affect the texture of the final dish.
- For a creamier texture, add a splash of low-fat milk or a dollop of plain low-fat Greek yogurt after cooking.
- If you don't have apples, you can substitute with other diced fruits suitable for the DASH diet, such as pears, peaches, or berries.
- To add a touch of sweetness without processed sugar, drizzle a little maple syrup or honey on top before serving (be mindful of portion size).

Raspberry Yogurt Cereal Bowl

This refreshing and satisfying raspberry yogurt cereal bowl is a perfect twist on a classic breakfast option for the DASH diet. Packed with protein and probiotics from Greek yogurt, fiber from bran flakes, and naturally sweet raspberries, it delivers a delicious and nutritious start to your day while keeping sodium in check.

 **Prep Time:** 5 minutes || **Cook Time:** No cook || **Yield:** 1 serving

INGREDIENTS
- 1 cup plain, low-fat Greek yogurt
- ½ cup unsweetened almond milk (or low-fat dairy milk)
- ½ cup bran flakes (or another whole-grain, low-sodium cereal)
- ½ cup fresh raspberries
- ¼ cup chopped walnuts or pecans (optional)
- 1 tablespoon ground flaxseed (optional)
- ½ teaspoon ground cinnamon
- Fresh mint leaves (optional, for garnish)

INSTRUCTIONS
1. In a bowl, whisk together the plain, low-fat Greek yogurt and unsweetened almond milk (or low-fat dairy milk) until smooth and creamy.
2. Add the bran flakes (or your chosen cereal) to the yogurt mixture. Top with the fresh raspberries.
3. Sprinkle with chopped walnuts or pecans and ground flaxseed (if using) for added protein, healthy fats, and fiber.
4. Dust with ground cinnamon for a touch of warmth and garnish with fresh mint leaves (optional) for a refreshing touch.

NOTES
- **Greek yogurt choice:** Opt for plain, low-fat Greek yogurt for the base. Flavored yogurts can be higher in sugar and sodium.
- **Sweetener options:** If desired, drizzle a touch of maple syrup or honey over the berries for additional sweetness, but be mindful of portion control.
- **Cereal options:** Choose a whole-grain, low-sodium cereal like bran flakes, shredded wheat, or check the sodium content of other options you prefer.
- **Leftovers:** While not ideal, leftover cereal and yogurt can be stored separately in airtight containers in the refrigerator for up to 1 day. However, the cereal might become soggy.

NUTRITIONAL INFORMATION (approximate per serving):
Calories: 300 | Protein: 20g | Fat: 10g (depending on nuts used) | Carbohydrates: 35g | Sodium: 180mg (depending on sodium content of yogurt and cereal) | Potassium: 500mg (depending on ingredients)

Sweet Potato Oat Waffles

These fluffy and flavorful sweet potato oat waffles are a perfect heart-healthy breakfast option for the DASH diet. Packed with fiber-rich oats and potassium-rich sweet potato, they offer a delicious and satisfying start to your day while keeping sodium in check.

Prep Time: 10 minutes || **Cook Time:** 15-20 minutes || **Yield:** 4 servings

INGREDIENTS

- 1 medium sweet potato (about 8 oz), peeled and diced
- 1 cup rolled oats
- 1 ½ tablespoons ground flaxseed
- 1 ½ cups unsweetened almond milk (or low-fat dairy milk)
- 1 egg white
- 1 teaspoon baking powder
- ½ teaspoon ground cinnamon
- ¼ teaspoon ground nutmeg
- Freshly ground black pepper to taste
- Cooking spray

INSTRUCTIONS

1. In a medium saucepan, cover the diced sweet potato with water and bring to a boil. Reduce heat and simmer for 10-12 minutes, or until tender. Drain the water and mash the sweet potato with a fork or potato masher until mostly smooth, leaving some small chunks for texture.
2. In a large bowl, whisk together the rolled oats, ground flaxseed, baking powder, cinnamon, nutmeg, and black pepper.
3. In a separate bowl, whisk together the unsweetened almond milk (or low-fat dairy milk) and egg white.
4. Add the mashed sweet potato to the dry ingredients and mix well. Then, pour in the wet ingredients and fold everything together until just combined. Be careful not to overmix.
5. Preheat your waffle iron. Lightly coat the waffle iron with cooking spray.
6. Pour about ½ cup of batter onto the preheated waffle iron for each waffle. Cook for 3-4 minutes, or until golden brown and crispy. The exact cooking time may vary depending on your waffle iron.
7. Serve the sweet potato oat waffles immediately while hot. You can enjoy them plain or top them with your favorite DASH-friendly options like:
   - Fresh berries (blueberries, raspberries, strawberries)
   - Sliced banana or apple
   - A dollop of low-fat Greek yogurt
   - A drizzle of low-sugar maple syrup or honey (use minimal amounts)

NOTES

- **Flaxseed meal alternative:** If you don't have ground flaxseed, you can substitute it with an equal amount of chia seeds or wheat germ.
- **Leftovers:** Leftover waffles can be stored in an airtight container in the refrigerator for up to 2 days. Reheat in a toaster or oven for a few minutes until warmed through.
- **Sodium content:** Be mindful of any added toppings, such as commercially prepared sauces or syrups, as they can be high in sodium. Choose fresh fruit or low-sodium options.

NUTRITIONAL INFORMATION (approximate per serving):

Calories: 250 | Protein: 6g | Fat: 5g | Carbohydrates: 40g | Sodium: 150mg (depending on sodium content of ingredients) | Potassium: 450mg (depending on ingredients)

Muesli Scones

These muesli scones offer a delicious and satisfying twist on a classic breakfast option for the DASH diet. Packed with fiber-rich oats and nuts from the muesli, whole-wheat flour, and a touch of fruit for sweetness, they deliver a nutritious start to your day while keeping sodium in check.

**Prep Time:** 15 minutes || **Cook Time:** 20-25 minutes || **Yield:** 6 scones

INGREDIENTS

- 1 ½ cups rolled oats (use a gluten-free variety if needed)
- ½ cup chopped nuts (almonds, pecans, or walnuts)
- ¼ cup dried cranberries or cherries (chopped)
- 1 ½ cups whole-wheat flour
- ½ teaspoon baking powder
- ¼ teaspoon baking soda
- ¼ teaspoon ground cinnamon
- ¼ teaspoon ground nutmeg
- Pinch of salt
- 1/3 cup low-fat ricotta cheese
- ¼ cup unsweetened almond milk (or low-fat dairy milk)
- 1 tablespoon honey or maple syrup
- 1 tablespoon melted unsalted butter (or coconut oil)
- 1 tablespoon chopped fresh orange zest (optional)

INSTRUCTIONS

1. Preheat your oven to 400°F (200°C). Line a baking sheet with parchment paper.
2. In a large bowl, whisk together the rolled oats, chopped nuts, dried cranberries or cherries (if using), whole-wheat flour, baking powder, baking soda, cinnamon, nutmeg, and salt.
3. In a separate bowl, whisk together the low-fat ricotta cheese, unsweetened almond milk (or low-fat dairy milk), honey or maple syrup, and melted butter (or coconut oil). Stir in the orange zest (if using).
4. Add the wet ingredients to the dry ingredients and mix with a spoon or spatula until just combined. Be careful not to overmix. The dough will be slightly sticky.
5. Turn the dough out onto a lightly floured surface and gently pat it down to a thickness of about 1 inch. Use a knife or bench scraper to cut the dough into 6 equal wedges (or desired shapes).
6. Transfer the scone wedges to the prepared baking sheet, leaving a little space between them for spreading. Bake for 20-25 minutes, or until golden brown.
7. Let the scones cool slightly on the baking sheet before transferring them to a wire rack to cool completely. Enjoy them warm or at room temperature.

NOTES

- **Muesli selection:** Choose a muesli that is low in added sugar and sodium. You can also make your own muesli by combining rolled oats, nuts, seeds, and dried fruit.
- **Sweetener options:** Honey or maple syrup add a touch of sweetness, but use them sparingly. You can experiment with other DASH-friendly sweeteners like stevia or monk fruit extract (adjust quantity based on sweetness level).

NUTRITIONAL INFORMATION (approximate per scone):

Calories: 250 | Protein: 5g | Fat: 10g (depending on fat source) | Carbohydrates: 35g | Sodium: 180mg (depending on sodium content of ingredients) | Potassium: 200mg (depending on ingredients)

Pumpkin Yogurt Parfait with Granola

This festive and flavorful pumpkin yogurt parfait is a perfect fall-inspired breakfast option for the DASH diet. Packed with protein and probiotics from Greek yogurt, fiber from bran flakes or whole-grain granola, and the natural sweetness of pumpkin puree, it delivers a delicious and nutritious start to your day while keeping sodium in check.

Prep Time: 5 minutes || **Cook Time:** No cook || **Yield:** 1 serving

INGREDIENTS
- 1 cup plain, low-fat Greek yogurt
- ½ cup unsweetened almond milk (or low-fat dairy milk)
- ½ cup pumpkin puree (canned unsweetened pumpkin puree is recommended)
- ¼ teaspoon ground cinnamon
- Pinch of ground nutmeg
- ¼ cup granola (preferably low-sodium and with whole grains like bran flakes)
- ¼ cup chopped walnuts or pecans (optional)
- Fresh mint leaves (optional, for garnish)

INSTRUCTIONS
1. In a bowl, whisk together the plain, low-fat Greek yogurt and unsweetened almond milk (or low-fat dairy milk) until smooth and creamy.
2. In the same bowl or a separate bowl, depending on preference for distinct layers, stir together the pumpkin puree, ground cinnamon, and nutmeg.
3. In a serving glass, start with a layer of the yogurt mixture. Top it with the pumpkin mixture.
4. Add a layer of granola. Sprinkle with chopped walnuts or pecans (if using) for added protein and healthy fats.
5. Decorate the top with a fresh mint leaf (optional) for a refreshing touch.

NOTES
- **Pumpkin puree selection:** Opt for canned unsweetened pumpkin puree, not pumpkin pie filling, to avoid added sugars.
- **Sweetener options:** This recipe relies on the natural sweetness of the pumpkin puree. If desired, add a drizzle of honey or maple syrup for additional sweetness, but use them sparingly.
- **Granola selection:** Choose a granola that is low in sodium and contains whole grains like bran flakes for added fiber. Consider making your own DASH-friendly granola to control ingredients.
- **Nut options:** Walnuts and pecans are good choices for added protein and healthy fats, but other unsalted nuts can be used as well.
- **Leftovers:** While not ideal, leftover parfait components can be stored separately in airtight containers in the refrigerator for up to 1 day. However, the granola might become soggy.

NUTRITIONAL INFORMATION (approximate per serving):
Calories: 350 | Protein: 20g (with nuts) | Fat: 12g (depending on nuts used) | Carbohydrates: 40g | Sodium: 180mg (depending on sodium content of ingredients) | Potassium: 500mg (depending on ingredients)

Buckwheat Crepes with Savory or Sweet Options

These versatile buckwheat crepes are perfect for the DASH diet! Buckwheat flour provides a good source of fiber and a naturally nutty flavor. The recipe is easily adaptable for both savory and sweet fillings, allowing you to create a satisfying and healthy breakfast, lunch, dinner, or snack. This recipe keeps sodium in check by using low-sodium ingredients and focusing on natural flavors.

 **Prep Time:** 10 minutes ||  **Cook Time:** 15-20 minutes (makes about 6 crepes) ||  **Yield:** Serves 2-3

INGREDIENTS
For the Basic Crepes:
- 1 cup buckwheat flour
- ¾ cup low-fat milk (or unsweetened plant-based milk alternative)
- 1 large egg
- ¼ cup water
- 1 tablespoon melted butter or olive oil
- Pinch of salt

INSTRUCTIONS
1. In a large bowl, whisk together the buckwheat flour and salt.
2. Create a well in the center of the dry ingredients.
3. In a separate bowl or measuring cup, whisk together the low-fat milk, egg, and water.
4. Slowly pour the wet ingredients into the well in the dry ingredients. Gradually whisk the wet ingredients into the dry ingredients, working from the center outwards until just combined. A few small lumps are okay. Do not overmix.
5. Stir in the melted butter or olive oil.
6. Heat a lightly oiled non-stick pan or griddle over medium heat.
7. For each crepe, pour about ⅓ cup of batter into the hot pan, tilting the pan to swirl the batter and create a thin, even layer.
8. Cook the crepe for 1-2 minutes, or until the edges begin to curl and the bottom is golden brown. Use a spatula to carefully loosen the edges and then flip the crepe. Cook for an additional 30 seconds to 1 minute, or until the other side is lightly golden brown.
9. Transfer the cooked crepe to a plate and cover it with a clean kitchen towel to keep it warm while you cook the remaining crepes.

NOTES
- **Resting the batter:** Letting the batter rest for 15-30 minutes before cooking allows the gluten in the buckwheat flour to relax, resulting in smoother and more tender crepes.
- **Adjusting consistency:** If the batter seems too thick, add a tablespoon or two of additional water or milk, one tablespoon at a time, until it reaches a pourable consistency. If the batter seems too thin, add a tablespoon or two of buckwheat flour until it thickens slightly.
- **Non-stick pan:** Using a non-stick pan helps prevent sticking and makes flipping the crepes easier.

Savory Crepe Options:
- **Spinach and Feta Filling:** Sauteed spinach with crumbled low-fat feta cheese, seasoned with black pepper and a squeeze of lemon juice.

- **Mushroom and Leek Filling:** Sauteed mushrooms and leeks with a touch of garlic and fresh herbs.
- **Smoked Salmon and Cream Cheese Filling:** Smoked salmon slices with a light schmear of low-fat cream cheese, topped with fresh dill and capers (optional).

Sweet Crepe Options:
- **Fresh Fruit and Yogurt Filling:** Sliced fresh fruit like berries or sliced banana with a dollop of plain, non-fat Greek yogurt and a drizzle of honey or maple syrup.
- **Lemon Ricotta Filling:** Ricotta cheese mixed with a squeeze of lemon juice and a touch of honey, topped with fresh lemon zest.
- **Apple Compote Filling:** Homemade or store-bought apple compote, warmed slightly for a gooey filling.

NUTRITIONAL INFORMATION (approximate per crepe without filling):
Calories: 150 | Protein: 5g | Fat: 5g | Carbohydrates: 20g | Sodium: 70mg (depending on sodium content of ingredients) | Potassium: 100mg (depending on ingredients)

Blueberry Yogurt Multigrain Pancakes

These fluffy and flavorful pancakes are a perfect fit for the DASH diet. Packed with protein-rich Greek yogurt and whole grains from the multigrain flour blend, they offer a satisfying and nutritious breakfast option. Bursting with fresh blueberries, these pancakes are naturally sweetened and keep sodium in check by using low-sodium ingredients.

 **Prep Time:** 10 minutes || **Cook Time:** 15-20 minutes || **Yield:** 4-5 pancakes

INGREDIENTS
For the Pancakes:
- 1 cup whole wheat and oat flour blend (or substitute with 1/2 cup whole wheat flour and 1/2 cup rolled oats)
- 2 teaspoons baking powder
- ½ teaspoon baking soda
- ½ teaspoon ground cinnamon
- Pinch of salt
- 1 cup plain, non-fat Greek yogurt
- ½ cup unsweetened almond milk (or low-fat milk)
- 1 large egg
- 1 tablespoon honey (or maple syrup)
- 1 teaspoon vanilla extract
- 1 cup fresh blueberries

INSTRUCTIONS
1. In a large bowl, whisk together the whole wheat and oat flour blend (or whole wheat flour and rolled oats), baking powder, baking soda, ground cinnamon, and salt.
2. In a separate bowl, whisk together the plain, non-fat Greek yogurt, almond milk (or low-fat milk), egg, honey (or maple syrup), and vanilla extract.
3. Pour the wet ingredients into the dry ingredients and stir gently with a spatula until just combined. Be careful not to overmix, as this can lead to tough pancakes.
4. Gently fold in the fresh blueberries using a rubber spatula. Avoid overmixing to prevent the blueberries from bursting.
5. Heat a lightly oiled griddle or non-stick pan over medium heat.
6. For each pancake, pour about ¼ cup of batter onto the hot griddle or pan.
7. Cook the pancakes for 2-3 minutes, or until bubbles appear on the surface and the edges begin to set. Use a spatula to carefully flip the pancakes.
8. Cook for an additional 1-2 minutes, or until the other side is golden brown and cooked through. Serve the pancakes immediately with your favorite toppings (see tips below).

NOTES
- **Flour options:** You can use a pre-made whole wheat and oat flour blend for convenience, or grind your own rolled oats into a flour consistency using a food processor or blender. If using only whole wheat flour, add an additional ¼ cup of rolled oats for texture.
- **Sweetener options:** Honey or maple syrup add a touch of sweetness to the pancakes. You can adjust the amount based on your preference or omit it entirely for a naturally sweetened option using the sweetness from the blueberries.
- **Milk options:** Unsweetened almond milk or low-fat milk can be used.
- **Toppings:** Top your pancakes with a dollop of plain, non-fat Greek yogurt, a drizzle of honey or maple syrup, and a sprinkle of fresh blueberries for a complete and satisfying breakfast. Chopped nuts like walnuts or pecans can also be added for extra texture and flavor.

NUTRITIONAL INFORMATION (approximate per pancake):
Calories: 250 | Protein: 10g | Fat: 5g | Carbohydrates: 40g | Sodium: 120mg (depending on sodium content of ingredients) | Potassium: 200mg (depending on ingredients)

Ezekiel Bread French Toast with Berries and Nut Butter

This delicious French toast recipe is a perfect way to incorporate sprouted grain bread, a mainstay of the DASH diet, into a satisfying breakfast. Ezekiel bread offers a complete protein source and additional fiber compared to regular white bread. The recipe uses low-sodium ingredients and natural sweetness from berries for a healthy and flavorful twist on a classic dish.

 **Prep Time:** 5 minutes || **Cook Time:** 10-12 minutes || **Yield:** 2 servings

INGREDIENTS

For the French Toast:
- 2 slices Ezekiel bread
- ½ cup unsweetened almond milk (or low-fat milk)
- 2 large eggs
- 1 teaspoon ground cinnamon
- ¼ teaspoon vanilla extract
- Pinch of salt (optional)

For the Toppings:
- 1 cup fresh berries (your choice or a mix)
- 2 tablespoons nut butter of your choice (almond, peanut, cashew)
- Optional: Maple syrup or honey (for a touch of additional sweetness)

INSTRUCTIONS

1. In a shallow dish or bowl, whisk together the unsweetened almond milk (or low-fat milk), eggs, ground cinnamon, vanilla extract, and a pinch of salt (optional) until well combined.
2. Heat a lightly oiled non-stick pan or griddle over medium heat.
3. Prepare the bread: While the pan heats, dip each slice of Ezekiel bread into the egg mixture, coating both sides evenly. Let the bread soak for a few seconds to allow some of the egg mixture to be absorbed.
4. Cook the French toast: Carefully transfer the soaked bread slices to the hot pan. Cook for 3-4 minutes per side, or until golden brown and cooked through.
5. Assemble and serve: Transfer the cooked French toast slices to plates. Top each slice with fresh berries and a dollop of nut butter. Drizzle with a touch of maple syrup or honey (optional) for additional sweetness. Enjoy!

NOTES

- **Ezekiel bread selection:** Choose your preferred variety of Ezekiel bread. They come in different grain combinations, such as sprouted wheat, barley, and lentils.
- **Milk options:** Unsweetened almond milk or low-fat milk can be used. If using dairy milk, opt for a low-fat or fat-free option to keep sodium in check.
- **Nut butter options:** Choose your favorite nut butter for the topping, such as almond butter, peanut butter, or cashew butter. Consider options with no added sugar or salt for a more DASH-friendly choice.
- **Berry options:** Any type of fresh berries will work well. You can use a single type of berry or a combination of your favorites for a colorful and flavorful topping.
- **Leftovers:** Leftover French toast can be stored in an airtight container in the refrigerator for up to 1 day. Reheat gently in a pan over medium heat or in the microwave until warmed through.

NUTRITIONAL INFORMATION (approximate per serving, without maple syrup or honey):

Calories: 350 | Protein: 15g | Fat: 15g | Carbohydrates: 40g | Sodium: 200mg (depending on sodium content of ingredients) | Potassium: 300mg (depending on ingredients)

Open-Faced Breakfast Sandwich with Avocado, Smoked Salmon, and Scrambled Eggs

This open-faced breakfast sandwich is a delightful and nutritious option for the DASH diet. Whole-wheat toast provides a source of fiber, while creamy avocado adds healthy fats and potassium. Smoked salmon offers a protein boost, and scrambled eggs complete the package with additional protein and essential nutrients. This recipe keeps sodium in check by using low-sodium smoked salmon and focusing on natural flavors.

 **Prep Time:** 5 minutes || **Cook Time:** 10-12 minutes || **Yield:** 1 serving

INGREDIENTS
For the Sandwich:
- 1 slice whole-wheat bread, toasted
- ½ ripe avocado, mashed
- 2 large eggs
- 1 tablespoon low-fat milk (or water)
- Pinch of dried thyme (optional)
- Salt and freshly ground black pepper (optional) to taste
- 2 ounces smoked salmon, thinly sliced

INSTRUCTIONS
1. Toast a slice of whole-wheat bread to your desired level of crispness.
2. While the bread toasts, mash half of a ripe avocado with a fork until creamy. Season with a pinch of salt and freshly ground black pepper (optional) to taste.
3. In a bowl, whisk together the eggs, low-fat milk (or water), and dried thyme (optional). Season with a pinch of salt and freshly ground black pepper (optional) to taste.
4. Heat a lightly oiled non-stick pan or skillet over medium heat. Once hot, pour in the whisked egg mixture. Use a rubber spatula to gently fold the eggs as they cook, scrambling them until they reach your desired consistency (soft scrambled, medium scrambled, etc.).
5. Spread the mashed avocado evenly over the toasted whole-wheat bread. Top with the scrambled eggs.
6. Arrange the thinly sliced smoked salmon on top of the scrambled eggs.
7. Enjoy your open-faced breakfast sandwich immediately.

NOTES
- **Bread options:** Choose a whole-wheat bread you enjoy, such as whole-wheat sourdough or whole-wheat Ezekiel bread.
- **Avocado ripeness:** For easier mashing, use a ripe avocado that yields to gentle pressure.
- **Herb options:** Dried thyme adds a subtle flavor to the scrambled eggs. You can substitute with other dried herbs like chives or dill if preferred.

Turkey, Bacon, and Egg Breakfast Tacos

These protein-packed breakfast tacos are a perfect fit for the DASH diet. Lean ground turkey and turkey bacon offer a lower-sodium alternative to traditional breakfast sausage, while whole-wheat tortillas provide a source of fiber. The recipe is rounded out with scrambled eggs, a touch of cheese, and fresh toppings like salsa and avocado for a satisfying and flavorful morning meal.

 **Prep Time:** 10 minutes || **Cook Time:** 15-20 minutes || **Yield:** 2 servings

INGREDIENTS

For the Tacos:
- 2 whole-wheat tortillas, warmed
- 4 ounces lean ground turkey
- 2 slices turkey bacon, chopped
- ½ cup chopped onion
- ½ green bell pepper, chopped (optional)
- 2 large eggs
- 1 tablespoon low-fat milk (or water)
- Pinch of dried oregano (optional)

- ¼ cup shredded low-fat cheddar cheese (or crumbled low-fat feta cheese)
- Salt and freshly ground black pepper (optional) to taste

For the Toppings (choose your favorites):
- Salsa
- Chopped avocado
- Low-fat Greek yogurt
- Chopped fresh cilantro

INSTRUCTIONS

1. Wrap the whole-wheat tortillas in a damp paper towel and heat them in the microwave for 30-60 seconds, or until warmed through and pliable. Alternatively, you can warm them in a dry skillet over low heat for a few seconds per side.
2. Heat a lightly oiled pan over medium heat. Add the ground turkey and cook, breaking it up with a spoon, until browned. Drain any excess grease. Add the chopped turkey bacon and cook for an additional minute or two, until crispy.
3. If using, add the chopped onion and green bell pepper to the pan with the cooked turkey and bacon. Sauté for 3-4 minutes, or until the vegetables are softened.
4. In a separate bowl, whisk together the eggs, low-fat milk (or water), and dried oregano (optional). Season with a pinch of salt and freshly ground black pepper (optional) to taste.
5. Push the cooked turkey, bacon, and vegetables (if using) to one side of the pan. Add the whisked egg mixture to the empty side of the pan and scramble the eggs until they reach your desired consistency (soft scrambled, medium scrambled, etc.). Once scrambled, fold in the cooked turkey, bacon, and vegetables (if using) to combine.
6. Place a warmed whole-wheat tortilla on a plate. Top with a scoop of the scrambled egg mixture with turkey and bacon (and vegetables, if using). Sprinkle with your desired amount of shredded low-fat cheddar cheese (or crumbled low-fat feta cheese).
7. Serve the breakfast tacos immediately with your favorite toppings like salsa, chopped avocado, low-fat Greek yogurt, and chopped fresh cilantro.

NOTES
- **Ground turkey selection**: Choose lean ground turkey (at least 90% lean) to limit fat content.
- **Turkey** bacon options: Look for turkey bacon labeled "low-sodium" or "no added salt" to keep sodium in check.
- **Milk options:** Low-fat milk or water can be used in the scrambled eggs. Water helps to keep sodium content low.

- **Cheese options:** Opt for low-fat cheddar cheese or crumbled low-fat feta cheese to add protein and flavor without excessive sodium.
- **Toppings:** Choose your favorite toppings to customize the flavor profile. Opt for fresh ingredients like salsa, avocado, and chopped cilantro for added nutrients and taste.

NUTRITIONAL INFORMATION (approximate per serving):
Calories: 400 | Protein: 25g | Fat: 15g | Carbohydrates: 30g | Sodium: 450mg (depending on sodium content of ingredients) | Potassium: 500mg (depending on ingredients)

Mushroom Spinach Omelet with Herbs

This protein-packed omelet filled with flavorful sauteed mushrooms and spinach, this recipe keeps sodium in check by using low-sodium ingredients and focusing on natural flavors from herbs and spices.

 **Prep Time:** 5 minutes || **Cook Time:** 10-12 minutes || **Yield:** 1 serving

INGREDIENTS
For the Omelet:
- 2 large eggs
- 1 tablespoon low-fat milk (or water)
- Pinch of dried thyme (optional)
- Pinch of dried parsley (optional)
- Salt and freshly ground black pepper (optional) to taste
- ½ cup chopped fresh mushrooms (cremini, portobello, or your choice)

- 1 cup fresh spinach, chopped

For Serving (optional):
- 1 tablespoon crumbled low-fat feta cheese (optional)
- Fresh herbs like chopped chives or parsley (optional)

INSTRUCTIONS
1. In a bowl, whisk together the eggs, low-fat milk (or water), dried thyme (optional), dried parsley (optional), salt, and freshly ground black pepper (optional) to taste.
2. Heat a lightly oiled non-stick pan or skillet over medium heat.
3. Add the chopped mushrooms to the hot pan and cook for 2-3 minutes, or until softened and slightly browned.
4. Add the chopped spinach to the pan with the cooked mushrooms. Cook for an additional minute or two, or until the spinach wilts.
5. Carefully pour the whisked egg mixture into the pan with the cooked mushrooms and spinach. Tilt the pan slightly to allow the egg to spread evenly.
6. As the eggs begin to set around the edges, use a rubber spatula to gently push the cooked egg towards the center of the pan, allowing the uncooked egg to flow underneath. Continue cooking for a few minutes, or until the desired level of doneness is reached (soft scrambled in the center, or cooked through).
7. If using, sprinkle crumbled low-fat feta cheese over one half of the omelet. Use a spatula to carefully fold the other half of the omelet over the filling.
8. Slide the cooked omelet onto a plate. Garnish with fresh herbs like chopped chives or parsley (optional) and enjoy immediately.

NOTES
- **Spinach variation:** Frozen chopped spinach, thawed and squeezed to remove excess moisture, can be used instead of fresh spinach.
- **Low-fat feta cheese:** Crumbled low-fat feta cheese adds a touch of creaminess and salty flavor. You can omit it entirely if you prefer a lower-sodium option.
- **Folding technique:** If you're new to making omelets, don't worry about achieving a perfect fold. You can simply cook the omelet until mostly set and then enjoy it open-faced.

NUTRITIONAL INFORMATION (approximate per serving, without feta cheese):
Calories: 250 | Protein: 15g | Fat: 10g | Carbohydrates: 5g | Sodium: 120mg (depending on sodium content of ingredients) | Potassium: 400mg (depending on ingredients)

Peanut Butter Banana Cinnamon Toast with Sliced Almonds

This recipe takes a classic favorite, peanut butter banana toast, and gives it a DASH-friendly makeover. Here, we focus on using low-sodium ingredients and adding potassium-rich bananas and almonds for a satisfying and nutritious breakfast option.

Prep Time: 5 minutes || **Cook Time:** 2-3 minutes || **Yield:** 1 serving

INGREDIENTS

For the Toast:
- 1 slice whole-wheat bread
- ½ tablespoon unsalted peanut butter (creamy or chunky)
- ½ small banana, sliced
- Pinch of ground cinnamon

For the Topping (optional):
- 1 tablespoon sliced almonds

INSTRUCTIONS

1. Toast the slice of whole-wheat bread in a toaster until golden brown and slightly crisp.
2. While the bread is hot, spread the unsalted peanut butter evenly over the toast.
3. Arrange the sliced banana on top of the peanut butter.
4. Sprinkle a pinch of ground cinnamon over the banana slices.
5. Enjoy your peanut butter banana cinnamon toast immediately.

NOTES

- **Peanut butter selection:** Look for unsalted peanut butter with minimal added ingredients.
- **Banana ripeness:** A ripe banana will have a sweeter flavor and a softer texture, making it easier to spread.
- **Toppings:** For added crunch and a touch of healthy fat, sprinkle with a tablespoon of sliced almonds. Chopped walnuts or pecans can be used as well.
- **Spice variation:** You can add a pinch of ground nutmeg or a sprinkle of chia seeds for a flavor twist.

NUTRITIONAL INFORMATION (approximate per serving):

Calories: 250 | Protein: 8g | Fat: 10g | Carbohydrates: 30g | Sodium: 120mg (depending on sodium content of peanut butter) | Potassium: 400mg (depending on ingredients)

Yogurt Parfait with Berries, Granola, and Chia Seeds

This vibrant parfait offers a layered and satisfying breakfast option that fits perfectly into the DASH diet. Packed with protein and fiber from Greek yogurt, berries, and granola, this recipe keeps sodium in check and focuses on natural sweetness from the fruit.

 **Prep Time:** 5 minutes || **Yield:** 1 serving

INGREDIENTS
- ½ cup plain, non-fat Greek yogurt
- ½ cup fresh or frozen mixed berries (blueberries, raspberries, strawberries)
- ¼ cup granola (low-sugar or homemade)
- 1 tablespoon chia seeds
- Fresh mint sprig (optional, for garnish)

INSTRUCTIONS
1. In a small bowl or parfait glass, layer half of the plain, non-fat Greek yogurt. Top with half of the fresh or frozen mixed berries.
2. Sprinkle half of the granola and half of the chia seeds over the berries.
3. Repeat the layers of yogurt, berries, granola, and chia seeds.
4. Garnish with a fresh mint sprig (optional) and enjoy immediately.

NOTES
- **Greek yogurt selection:** Opt for plain, non-fat Greek yogurt for a base that's lower in sugar and sodium. You can add a drizzle of honey or maple syrup for a touch of sweetness, but use them sparingly.
- **Berry options:** Choose your favorite berries or a mix for variety. Frozen berries can be used, but thaw them slightly before assembling the parfait.
- **Granola selection:** Look for low-sugar granola or make your own using rolled oats, nuts, seeds, and a touch of honey or maple syrup.
- **Chia seed benefits:** Chia seeds add a boost of fiber and healthy fats to the parfait. They also absorb liquid and take on a gel-like texture, adding a satisfying element to the dish.

NUTRITIONAL INFORMATION (approximate per serving):
Calories: 300 | Protein: 15g | Fat: 5g | Carbohydrates: 40g | Sodium: 80mg (depending on sodium content of yogurt and granola) | Potassium: 450mg (depending on ingredients)

Herbed Wild Mushroom Oatmeal with Flaxseed Meal

This flavorful oatmeal boasts a satisfying combination of textures and tastes, making it a perfect breakfast option for the DASH diet. Earthy wild mushrooms and fresh herbs add depth of flavor, while flaxseed meal provides a boost of fiber and healthy fats. This recipe focuses on low-sodium ingredients and keeps added sugar in check.

 **Prep Time:** 5 minutes || **Cook Time:** 15-20 minutes || **Yield:** 1 serving

INGREDIENTS

For the Oatmeal:
- ½ cup rolled oats (old-fashioned or quick oats)
- 1 cup low-sodium vegetable broth
- ½ cup water
- 1 tablespoon ground flaxseed meal
- Pinch of salt (optional)

For the Sautéed Mushrooms:
- 1 tablespoon olive oil
- ½ cup chopped wild mushrooms (cremini, portobello, or your choice)
- ¼ cup chopped onion
- 1 clove garlic, minced
- ½ teaspoon dried thyme
- Pinch of freshly ground black pepper

For Serving (optional):
- Chopped fresh herbs like parsley, chives, or dill
- Sliced almonds or walnuts (optional)

INSTRUCTIONS

1. In a medium saucepan, combine the rolled oats, low-sodium vegetable broth, water, ground flaxseed meal, and a pinch of salt (optional).
2. Bring the mixture to a simmer over medium heat.
3. Reduce heat to low, cover the pan, and simmer for 15-20 minutes, or until the oats are cooked through and have a creamy consistency, stirring occasionally.
4. While the oatmeal cooks, heat olive oil in a separate skillet over medium heat. Add the chopped wild mushrooms, chopped onion, and minced garlic. Sauté for 5-7 minutes, or until the vegetables are softened and the mushrooms are lightly browned.
5. Stir in the dried thyme and a pinch of freshly ground black pepper.
6. Ladle the cooked oatmeal into a bowl. Top with the sautéed wild mushrooms and sprinkle with chopped fresh herbs like parsley, chives, or dill (optional). For added crunch, you can also sprinkle with sliced almonds or walnuts (optional).

NOTES
- **Flaxseed meal:** Flaxseed meal adds fiber and healthy fats to the oatmeal. You can grind whole flaxseeds in a spice grinder or coffee grinder just before using for the freshest flavor.
- **Herb variations:** Experiment with different fresh herbs like parsley, chives, dill, or a combination for a variety of flavors.
- **Leftovers:** Leftover oatmeal can be stored in an airtight container in the refrigerator for up to 2 days. Reheat gently on the stovetop or in the microwave until warmed through.

NUTRITIONAL INFORMATION (approximate per serving):
Calories: 300 | Protein: 8g | Fat: 10g | Carbohydrates: 40g | Sodium: 150mg (depending on sodium content of broth) | Potassium: 400mg (depending on ingredients)

Ricotta and Pomegranate Bruschetta with Balsamic Glaze

This vibrant bruschetta recipe offers a light and flavorful appetizer or snack that perfectly fits the DASH diet. Creamy ricotta cheese is balanced by the tart sweetness of pomegranate arils, while a balsamic glaze adds a touch of acidity without excessive sodium.

 **Prep Time:** 15 minutes || **Yield:** 4 servings

INGREDIENTS
For the Bruschetta:
- 1 baguette, sliced into ½-inch thick slices
- 1 tablespoon olive oil
- ½ cup ricotta cheese (part-skim or low-fat)
- ½ cup pomegranate arils
- ¼ cup chopped fresh basil
- Pinch of freshly ground black pepper (optional)

For the Balsamic Glaze (optional):
- ¼ cup balsamic vinegar
- 1 tablespoon brown sugar (or honey)

INSTRUCTIONS
1. Preheat your oven to 400°F (200°C).
2. Brush the baguette slices with olive oil. Arrange the slices on a baking sheet and bake in the preheated oven for 5-7 minutes, or until golden brown and slightly crispy.
3. While the bread toasts, combine the part-skim or low-fat ricotta cheese, pomegranate arils, and chopped fresh basil in a small bowl. Stir gently to combine.
4. In a small saucepan, combine balsamic vinegar and brown sugar (or honey). Heat over medium heat, stirring occasionally, until the mixture simmers and thickens slightly, about 5-7 minutes. Remove from heat and let cool slightly. Note: Balsamic glaze is optional, and you can skip this step if preferred.
5. Spread the ricotta cheese mixture evenly over the toasted baguette slices. Top with a sprinkle of freshly ground black pepper (optional). Drizzle with balsamic glaze (optional) and serve immediately.

NOTES
- **Balsamic glaze alternative:** If skipping the balsamic glaze, you can drizzle the bruschetta with a touch of high-quality olive oil for extra flavor.
- **Bread selection:** Choose a whole-wheat baguette for added fiber, or use a gluten-free alternative if needed.
- **Ricotta cheese:** Opt for part-skim or low-fat ricotta cheese to keep saturated fat in check.
- **Pomegranate arils:** You can find pomegranate arils pre-packaged in most grocery stores, or separate them from a fresh pomegranate yourself.
- Leftovers: Leftover ricotta cheese mixture can be stored in an airtight container in the refrigerator for up to 2 days. However, assembled bruschetta is best enjoyed fresh.

NUTRITIONAL INFORMATION (approximate per serving, without balsamic glaze):
Calories: 250 | Protein: 8g | Fat: 10g | Carbohydrates: 30g | Sodium: 200mg (depending on sodium content of ingredients) | Potassium: 300mg (depending on ingredients)

Asparagus Omelet Tortilla Wrap with Lemon and Feta

This protein-packed wrap is a perfect addition to the DASH diet. A fluffy omelet filled with tender asparagus and crumbled feta cheese is wrapped in a whole-wheat tortilla, offering a satisfying and flavorful low-sodium meal.

**Prep Time:** 10 minutes || **Cook Time:** 15-20 minutes || **Yield:** 1 serving

INGREDIENTS

For the Omelet:
- 2 large eggs
- 1 tablespoon unsweetened almond milk (or low-fat milk)
- Pinch of dried thyme
- Pinch of garlic powder
- Salt and freshly ground black pepper (optional, to taste)

- 1 tablespoon olive oil

For the Filling:
- 4-5 asparagus spears, trimmed and cut into bite-sized pieces
- ¼ cup crumbled low-fat feta cheese

- 1 tablespoon chopped fresh parsley

For the Wrap:
- 1 whole-wheat tortilla (large size)

Optional Garnish:
- Lemon wedges

INSTRUCTIONS

1. Wash and trim the asparagus spears. Cut them into bite-sized pieces.
2. In a bowl, whisk together the eggs, almond milk (or milk), dried thyme, garlic powder, and a pinch of salt and freshly ground black pepper (optional, to taste).
3. Heat a small skillet over medium heat. Add a drizzle of olive oil and cook the asparagus pieces for 2-3 minutes, or until tender-crisp.
4. In the same skillet (or a larger nonstick skillet if needed), add the remaining olive oil and heat it over medium heat. Pour in the whisked egg mixture and tilt the pan to spread the eggs evenly. Let the omelet cook for 1-2 minutes, or until the bottom starts to set.
5. Once the bottom of the omelet is set, sprinkle the cooked asparagus pieces and crumbled feta cheese over one half of the omelet.
6. Using a spatula, carefully fold the other half of the omelet over the filling. Cook for an additional minute or two, or until the omelet is cooked through.
7. Briefly warm the whole-wheat tortilla in a dry skillet or microwave (wrapped in a paper towel) to make it more pliable.
8. Place the cooked omelet on the warmed tortilla. Sprinkle with chopped fresh parsley.
9. Fold the tortilla around the omelet filling to create a wrap. Serve immediately with lemon wedges for squeezing additional fresh lemon juice over the wrap if desired.

NOTES
- **Egg substitutes:** For a vegan option, you can use a ¼ cup of chickpea flour mixed with ¼ cup of water instead of eggs. Whisk this mixture well before adding it to the pan.
- **Cheese alternatives:** If feta cheese is not available, you can substitute it with a sprinkle of grated Parmesan cheese or crumbled low-fat ricotta cheese.
- **Leftovers:** Leftover omelet filling can be stored in an airtight container in the refrigerator for up to 1 day. Reheat gently on the stovetop and assemble a fresh wrap when ready to serve.

NUTRITIONAL INFORMATION (approximate per serving):
Calories: 350 | Protein: 20g | Fat: 15g | Carbohydrates: 25g | Sodium: 400mg (depending on sodium content of ingredients) | Potassium: 500mg (depending on ingredients)

Black Bean and White Cheddar Frittata with Fresh Herbs

This vibrant black bean and white cheddar frittata offers a flavorful and satisfying breakfast or brunch option that perfectly fits the DASH diet. Packed with protein-rich black beans and creamy white cheddar cheese, it's baked to golden perfection in a single skillet. This recipe keeps sodium content in check by using low-sodium ingredients and fresh herbs.

 **Prep Time:** 10 minutes || **Cook Time:** 20-25 minutes || **Yield:** 4 servings

INGREDIENTS
For the Frittata:
- 8 large eggs
- ¼ cup low-fat milk (or unsweetened almond milk)
- Pinch of dried oregano
- Pinch of garlic powder
- Pinch of freshly ground black pepper
- Salt (optional, to taste)
- 1 tablespoon olive oil
- ½ cup chopped red onion
- 1 cup drained and rinsed black beans
- ½ cup crumbled low-fat white cheddar cheese
- ¼ cup chopped fresh cilantro
- ¼ cup chopped fresh parsley

INSTRUCTIONS
1. Preheat your oven to 375°F (190°C). Lightly grease a 9-inch oven-safe skillet or pie dish.
2. In a large bowl, whisk together the eggs, low-fat milk (or almond milk), dried oregano, garlic powder, and black pepper. Add a pinch of salt (optional) to taste.
3. Heat olive oil in the preheated skillet over medium heat. Add the chopped red onion and cook for 2-3 minutes, or until softened.
4. Add the cooked onion and drained black beans to the whisked egg mixture. Stir in the crumbled low-fat white cheddar cheese, chopped fresh cilantro, and chopped fresh parsley. Pour the mixture into the greased skillet.
5. Bake the frittata in the preheated oven for 20-25 minutes, or until the eggs are set and the center is no longer jiggly. A toothpick inserted into the center should come out clean.
6. Let the frittata cool slightly before cutting into wedges. Serve warm or at room temperature.

NOTES
- **Vegetable variations:** You can add other chopped vegetables to the frittata, such as bell peppers, mushrooms, or spinach. Saute them with the onion before adding them to the egg mixture.
- **Herb variations:** Chopped chives, dill, or basil can be used instead of cilantro and parsley.
- **Cheese alternatives:** If white cheddar cheese is not available, you can substitute it with another low-fat cheese like crumbled low-fat mozzarella or Monterey Jack.

Almond Chai Granola with Low-Sodium Spices

This flavorful almond chai granola offers a delicious and healthy breakfast option that perfectly fits the DASH diet. Whole grain oats and nuts are coated in a fragrant chai spice mixture with a touch of maple syrup for sweetness, keeping sodium content in check while boasting warm and aromatic chai flavors.

 **Prep Time:** 10 minutes || **Cook Time:** 30-35 minutes || **Yield:** 6-8 servings

INGREDIENTS
- 4 cups rolled oats (old-fashioned or quick oats)
- 1 cup chopped almonds
- ½ cup sliced or slivered natural almonds (for topping)
- ¼ cup chopped walnuts (optional)
- ¼ cup unsweetened shredded coconut (optional)
- 2 tablespoons chia seeds
- 1 tablespoon ground flaxseed (optional)
- 2 tablespoons olive oil
- ¼ cup pure maple syrup
- 1 teaspoon ground cinnamon
- ½ teaspoon ground ginger
- ½ teaspoon ground cardamom
- ¼ teaspoon ground nutmeg
- Pinch of ground cloves (optional)
- Pinch of salt (optional)

INSTRUCTIONS
1. Preheat your oven to 325°F (165°C). Line a large baking sheet with parchment paper.
2. In a large bowl, combine the rolled oats, chopped almonds, sliced or slivered natural almonds (for topping), chopped walnuts (optional), unsweetened shredded coconut (optional), and chia seeds.
3. If using flaxseed, grind it in a spice grinder or coffee grinder. Add the ground flaxseed to the dry ingredient mixture in the bowl.
4. In a small bowl, whisk together the olive oil, maple syrup, ground cinnamon, ground ginger, ground cardamom, ground nutmeg, and a pinch of ground cloves (optional). Add a pinch of salt (optional) to taste.
5. Pour the wet ingredients over the dry ingredients in the large bowl. Stir well to coat the oat mixture evenly with the spices and sweetener.
6. Spread the coated oat mixture evenly on the prepared baking sheet.
7. Bake the granola in the preheated oven for 20-25 minutes, stirring occasionally, until the oats are golden brown and crispy.
8. In the last 5 minutes of baking, sprinkle the top of the granola with the sliced or slivered natural almonds (for topping). This will toast the almonds and add an extra layer of crunch.
9. Remove the granola from the oven and let it cool completely on the baking sheet. The granola will crisp up further as it cools.
10. Store the cooled almond chai granola in an airtight container at room temperature for up to a week. Enjoy it as a breakfast cereal with low-fat milk or yogurt, or as a topping for yogurt parfaits and fruit salads.

NOTES
- **Spice variations:** You can adjust the amount of spices to your preference. For a stronger chai flavor, add a bit more ground ginger or cardamom.
- **Sweetener variations:** You can substitute the maple syrup with another liquid sweetener like honey or agave nectar. Adjust the amount to your taste preference.

- **Nut and seed variations:** Feel free to adjust the nuts and seeds in this recipe. Use other chopped nuts like pecans or hazelnuts, or substitute sunflower seeds for the chia seeds.
- **Serving variations:** For an extra protein boost, sprinkle the granola with a touch of chopped dried fruit or shredded low-fat cheese before serving.

NUTRITIONAL INFORMATION (approximate per serving):
Calories: 300 | Protein: 5g | Fat: 15g | Carbohydrates: 35g | Sodium: 30mg (depending on sodium content of ingredients) | Potassium: 200mg (depending on ingredients)

PART THREE

SOUPS & SALADS

French Onion Soup

This flavorful French onion soup is a satisfying and heart-healthy option that fits perfectly with the DASH diet. It's lower in sodium and fat compared to traditional recipes, but still delivers that rich, caramelized onion taste.

 **Prep Time:** 10 minutes || **Cook Time:** 45 minutes || **Yield:** 4 servings

INGREDIENTS
- 2 teaspoons olive oil
- 5 large yellow onions, thinly sliced
- 6 cups low-sodium beef broth
- 2 cups water
- 2 tablespoons fresh thyme leaves
- 2 bay leaves
- 1/4 teaspoon freshly ground black pepper
- 1/4 cup grated Parmesan cheese
- 4 slices whole-wheat bread, toasted

INSTRUCTIONS
1. Heat olive oil in a large Dutch oven or heavy-bottomed pot over medium heat. Add the onions and cook, stirring occasionally, until softened and translucent, about 10 minutes.
2. Reduce heat to low and continue cooking the onions, stirring frequently, for 30-35 minutes, or until deeply caramelized and golden brown. Be patient, this step takes time but creates the rich flavor base.
3. Add the low-sodium beef broth, water, thyme, bay leaves, and black pepper. Increase heat to medium-high and bring to a boil. Reduce heat to low, cover, and simmer for 20 minutes.
4. Remove bay leaves and discard. Preheat broiler to high.
5. Divide the soup among 4 oven-safe bowls. Top each bowl with a toasted whole-wheat bread slice and sprinkle with Parmesan cheese.
6. Broil for 2-3 minutes, or until cheese is melted and bubbly. Watch closely to avoid burning.
7. Let cool slightly before serving.

NOTES
- Look for low-sodium beef broth to further reduce sodium content.
- You can substitute fresh thyme with 1 teaspoon dried thyme.
- For a thicker soup, remove 1/4 cup of cooked onions before adding the broth. Mash the reserved onions with a fork and stir them back into the soup for a richer texture.
- For a vegetarian option, use vegetable broth instead of beef broth.
- Experiment with different types of cheese. Gruyere or mozzarella can be used in place of Parmesan.

NUTRITIONAL INFORMATION (approximate per serving):
Calories: 250 | Protein: 10 g | Fat: 10 g | Carbohydrates: 30 g | Sodium: 400mg (depending on sodium content of broth) | Potassium: 300mg (depending on ingredients)

Black Bean Salad

This refreshing and protein-packed black bean salad is a perfect side dish or light lunch option for the DASH diet. It's loaded with colorful vegetables, low in sodium, and bursting with flavor.

 **Prep Time:** 10 minutes ||  **Cook Time:** 10 minutes (optional) ||  **Yield:** 4-6 servings

INGREDIENTS
- 1 (15 oz) can low-sodium black beans, rinsed and drained
- 1 cup cherry tomatoes, halved
- 1 cup chopped cucumber
- ½ cup chopped red onion
- ½ cup chopped fresh corn (fresh off the cob or thawed frozen corn)
- ¼ cup chopped fresh cilantro
- 2 tablespoons olive oil
- 2 tablespoons fresh lime juice
- 1 tablespoon red wine vinegar (optional)
- 1 teaspoon ground cumin
- ½ teaspoon dried oregano
- Salt and freshly ground black pepper to taste
- ¼ cup crumbled feta cheese (optional)
- ¼ cup chopped fresh avocado (optional)

INSTRUCTIONS
1. If using fresh corn, cook it in a pot of boiling water for 5-7 minutes, or until tender. Drain and cool slightly. You can also use frozen corn, thawed and patted dry.
2. In a large bowl, combine the black beans, cherry tomatoes, cucumber, red onion, and corn (if using).
3. In a small bowl, whisk together the olive oil, lime juice, red wine vinegar (if using), cumin, and oregano. Season with salt and pepper to taste.
4. Pour the dressing over the salad ingredients and toss gently to coat.
5. Divide the salad among plates and garnish with fresh cilantro. Optionally, crumble feta cheese and top the salad or add chopped avocado for extra creaminess.

NOTES
- Look for pre-washed and chopped vegetables to save time on prepping.
- If you don't have fresh corn, canned corn (drained and rinsed) can be used in a pinch.
- Adjust the amount of lime juice and red wine vinegar to your taste preference.
- For a spicier salad, add a pinch of red pepper flakes or chopped jalapeño pepper to the dressing.
- This salad is even more flavorful if chilled for at least 30 minutes before serving.
- Leftovers can be stored in an airtight container in the refrigerator for up to 3 days.

NUTRITIONAL INFORMATION (approximate per serving, without optional toppings):
Calories: 200 | Protein: 8g | Fat: 8g | Carbohydrates: 25g | Sodium: 300mg (depending on sodium content of ingredients) | Potassium: 500mg (depending on ingredients)

Low-Sodium Egg Salad

This protein-packed egg salad is a delicious and satisfying lunch option that fits perfectly with the DASH diet. Made with low-sodium ingredients and flavorful alternatives, it delivers classic taste without the excess sodium.

 **Prep Time:** 10 minutes || **Cook Time:** 10 minutes || **Yield:** 2-3 servings

INGREDIENTS
- 4 hard-boiled eggs, peeled and chopped
- ¼ cup chopped celery
- ¼ cup chopped red onion
- 2 tablespoons low-fat plain Greek yogurt
- 1 tablespoon Dijon mustard
- 1 tablespoon chopped fresh dill
- 1 tablespoon lemon juice
- ¼ teaspoon freshly ground black pepper
- Pinch of paprika (optional)
- Lettuce leaves or whole-wheat bread slices for serving

INSTRUCTIONS
1. Place the hard-boiled eggs in a medium bowl and chop them with a knife or egg slicer.
2. Add the chopped celery, red onion, Greek yogurt, Dijon mustard, dill, lemon juice, and black pepper to the bowl with the eggs.
3. Gently fold all the ingredients together until well combined. Be careful not to overmix, as the egg salad can become mushy.
4. Taste and adjust seasonings as needed. You may want to add a pinch of salt substitute or additional lemon juice for a brighter flavor profile.

NOTES
- To make perfectly hard-boiled eggs, place them in a single layer in a saucepan and cover with cold water. Bring to a boil, then remove from heat and let sit for 10-12 minutes. Drain and rinse with cold water to stop the cooking process. Peel and chop the eggs when cool enough to handle.
- Look for low-sodium or no-salt-added options for Greek yogurt and Dijon mustard to further reduce sodium content.
- If the mixture seems dry, add a teaspoon of low-fat mayonnaise or mashed avocado for extra creaminess.
- For a vegetarian option, substitute mashed chickpeas or lentils for some of the chopped eggs.
- Serve the egg salad on lettuce leaves for a low-carb option, or use whole-wheat bread slices for a heartier meal.

NUTRITIONAL INFORMATION (approximate per serving):
Calories: 200 | Protein: 12g | Fat: 5g | Carbohydrates: 15g | Sodium: 150mg (depending on sodium content of ingredients) | Potassium: 200mg (depending on ingredients)

Mulligatawny Soup

This flavorful Mulligatawny soup is a delicious and satisfying option for the DASH diet. It's been lightened up with lower-sodium ingredients and vegetable broth, but still delivers the rich and aromatic taste of the classic recipe.

**Prep Time:** 15 minutes || **Cook Time:** 45 minutes || **Yield:** 4-6 servings

INGREDIENTS
- 1 tablespoon olive oil
- 1 large onion, chopped
- 2 carrots, chopped
- 1 celery stalk, chopped
- 1 clove garlic, minced
- 1 teaspoon ground turmeric
- ½ teaspoon ground cumin
- ¼ teaspoon ground coriander
- Pinch of cayenne pepper (optional)
- 4 cups low-sodium vegetable broth
- 1 (15 oz) can diced tomatoes, fire-roasted preferred (undrained)
- 1 (15 oz) can chickpeas, rinsed and drained
- 1 cup chopped red lentils (rinsed)
- 1 cup chopped cooked chicken breast or shredded tofu (optional, for added protein)
- ½ cup chopped fresh cilantro
- Salt and freshly ground black pepper to taste
- 1 cup chopped cooked brown rice (optional)
- ¼ cup chopped cashews or peanuts (optional, for garnish)

INSTRUCTIONS
1. Heat olive oil in a large Dutch oven or pot over medium heat. Add the chopped onion, carrots, and celery. Cook for 5-7 minutes, or until softened and translucent.
2. Stir in the garlic, turmeric, cumin, coriander, and cayenne pepper (if using). Cook for an additional minute, allowing the spices to release their fragrance.
3. Pour in the low-sodium vegetable broth and diced tomatoes with their juices. Bring to a boil, then reduce heat and simmer for 15 minutes.
4. Add the rinsed lentils and chickpeas to the pot. Simmer for an additional 15-20 minutes, or until the lentils are tender.
5. If using chicken or tofu, add it to the soup during the last 5 minutes of cooking.
6. Season with salt and freshly ground black pepper to taste. Start with a small amount of salt and gradually add more to avoid over-salting.
7. Stir in the chopped fresh cilantro just before serving.

NOTES
- Look for low-sodium vegetable broth to further reduce sodium content.
- For a thicker soup, mash about ¼ cup of cooked lentils with a fork before adding them back to the pot for a richer texture.
- To make the soup vegan, omit the chicken and use vegetable broth.
- Serve the soup with a side of chopped cooked brown rice for a complete and satisfying meal (optional).

NUTRITIONAL INFORMATION (approximate per serving, without optional chicken, brown rice, and cashews):
Calories: 300 | Protein: 12g (with chicken) or 8g (without chicken) | Fat: 10g | Carbohydrates: 40g | Sodium: 400mg (depending on sodium content of ingredients) | Potassium: 500mg (depending on ingredients)

Turkey and Vegetable Barley Soup

This hearty and flavorful turkey and vegetable barley soup is a perfect addition to your DASH diet meal plan. Packed with lean protein from turkey, fiber-rich vegetables and barley, it's a nourishing and satisfying soup that keeps sodium in check.

 **Prep Time:** 15 minutes || **Cook Time:** 30-35 minutes || **Yield:** 4 servings

INGREDIENTS
- 1 tablespoon olive oil
- 1 medium onion, chopped
- 2 carrots, chopped
- 2 celery stalks, chopped
- 2 cloves garlic, minced
- 4 cups reduced-sodium chicken broth
- 4 cups water
- ½ cup quick-cooking barley
- 2 cups chopped cooked turkey breast
- 1 (14.5 oz) can diced tomatoes, undrained (fire-roasted or petite diced recommended)
- 1 cup frozen peas
- 1 cup chopped spinach or kale
- ½ teaspoon dried thyme
- ¼ teaspoon dried rosemary
- Pinch of black pepper
- Chopped fresh parsley (optional, for garnish)

INSTRUCTIONS
1. Heat the olive oil in a large pot or Dutch oven over medium heat. Add the chopped onion, carrots, and celery. Sauté for 5-7 minutes, or until softened.
2. Stir in the minced garlic and cook for an additional 30 seconds, until fragrant.
3. Add the reduced-sodium chicken broth, water, and quick-cooking barley to the pot. Bring to a boil, then reduce heat to simmer.
4. Simmer for 15 minutes, or until the barley is almost cooked through.
5. Add the cooked turkey breast and diced tomatoes with their juices to the pot. Stir to combine.
6. Add the frozen peas and chopped spinach or kale to the pot. Cook for an additional 2-3 minutes, or until the peas are warmed through and the greens are wilted.
7. Stir in the dried thyme, dried rosemary, and black pepper. Season with a touch of salt (optional), if needed, considering the sodium content of the broth and tomatoes.
8. Ladle the hot turkey and vegetable barley soup into bowls and garnish with chopped fresh parsley (optional). Serve with a whole-wheat bread roll for a complete meal.

NOTES
- **Pre-cooked turkey:** Using leftover cooked turkey breast or rotisserie chicken is a great time-saver for this recipe.
- **Vegetable options:** Feel free to add other chopped vegetables to the soup, such as green beans, zucchini, or chopped mushrooms.
- **Barley types:** You can substitute quick-cooking barley with pearl barley, but adjust the cooking time, as pearl barley takes longer to cook.
- **Leftovers:** Leftover soup can be stored in an airtight container in the refrigerator for up to 3 days. Reheat gently on the stovetop over low heat until warmed through.

NUTRITIONAL INFORMATION (approximate per serving):
Calories: 350 | Protein: 30g | Fat: 10g | Carbohydrates: 35g | Sodium: 400mg (depending on sodium content of ingredients) | Potassium: 700mg (depending on ingredients)

Turkish Red Lentil Soup (Kırmızı Mercimek Çorbası)

This flavorful Turkish red lentil soup is a perfect comfort food option for the DASH diet. Packed with protein and fiber-rich red lentils, colorful vegetables, and seasoned with a light tomato broth and a touch of lemon juice, it delivers a satisfying and nutritious meal that keeps sodium in check.

 **Prep Time:** 15 minutes || **Cook Time:** 30-35 minutes || **Yield:** 4 servings

INGREDIENTS

- 1 tablespoon olive oil
- 1 onion, finely chopped
- 2 carrots, coarsely grated
- 2 celery stalks, finely chopped (about 30g)
- 1 red bell pepper, finely chopped (optional)
- 2 garlic cloves, minced
- 1 cup red lentils, rinsed and drained
- 4 cups low-sodium vegetable broth
- 1 (14.5-oz) can diced tomatoes, undrained (fire-roasted tomatoes for added flavor)

- 1 teaspoon ground cumin
- ½ teaspoon dried thyme
- Pinch of red pepper flakes (optional, for a spicy kick)
- 1 tablespoon freshly squeezed lemon juice
- Salt and freshly ground black pepper to taste (optional)
- Chopped fresh parsley (optional, for garnish)

INSTRUCTIONS

1. Heat the olive oil in a large pot or Dutch oven over medium heat. Add the chopped onion, carrots, celery, and red bell pepper (if using). Sauté for 5-7 minutes, or until softened.
2. Stir in the minced garlic, ground cumin, dried thyme, and red pepper flakes (if using). Cook for an additional minute to release the fragrance of the spices.
3. Add the rinsed and drained red lentils, low-sodium vegetable broth, and diced tomatoes (undrained) to the pot. Bring to a boil, then reduce heat, cover, and simmer for 20-25 minutes, or until the lentils are tender and the soup has thickened slightly.
4. Stir in the freshly squeezed lemon juice. Taste the soup and adjust seasonings with salt and freshly ground black pepper (optional) as desired. Remember, the vegetable broth and tomatoes will contribute some sodium, so taste before adding additional salt.
5. Ladle the Turkish red lentil soup into bowls. Garnish with chopped fresh parsley (optional) and serve hot with a side of whole-wheat bread for dipping (optional).

NOTES

- **Vegetable options:** While the classic recipe includes onions, carrots, celery, and red bell pepper, you can customize the vegetables based on your preferences. Other DASH-friendly options include chopped zucchini, chopped green beans, or a handful of spinach added towards the end of cooking.
- **Tomato selection:** Fire-roasted tomatoes can add a smoky flavor to the soup, but any diced tomatoes will work. Opt for low-sodium canned tomatoes whenever possible.
- **Red pepper flakes:** The red pepper flakes are optional, but they add a touch of heat. Adjust the amount to your desired spice level.
- **Leftovers:** Leftover soup can be stored in an airtight container in the refrigerator for up to 3 days. Reheat gently in a pan over medium heat until warmed through.

NUTRITIONAL INFORMATION (approximate per serving):

Calories: 250 | Protein: 15g | Fat: 5g | Carbohydrates: 35g | Sodium: 400mg (depending on sodium content of ingredients) | Potassium: 500mg (depending on ingredients)

Quinoa and Vegetable Stew

This hearty and flavorful quinoa and vegetable stew is a perfect weeknight meal option for the DASH diet. Packed with protein and fiber-rich quinoa, a variety of colorful vegetables, and seasoned with a light tomato broth, it delivers a satisfying and nutritious dish that keeps sodium in check.

**Prep Time:** 15 minutes || **Cook Time:** 30-35 minutes || **Yield:** 4 servings

INGREDIENTS
- 1 cup rinsed quinoa
- 1 ½ cups low-sodium vegetable broth
- 1 tablespoon olive oil
- 1 cup chopped onion
- 1 clove garlic, minced
- 1 cup chopped carrots
- 1 cup chopped zucchini
- ½ cup chopped celery
- 1 (14.5-oz) can diced tomatoes, undrained (fire-roasted tomatoes for added flavor)
- ½ cup frozen peas
- 1 cup chopped fresh spinach or kale
- ½ teaspoon dried oregano
- ¼ teaspoon dried thyme
- Pinch of red pepper flakes (optional, for a spicy kick)
- Salt and freshly ground black pepper to taste (optional, adjust after taste test)
- Chopped fresh parsley (optional, for garnish)

INSTRUCTIONS
1. In a medium saucepan, combine the rinsed quinoa and low-sodium vegetable broth. Bring to a boil, then reduce heat, cover, and simmer for 15 minutes, or until the quinoa is cooked through and fluffy. Once cooked, remove from heat and set aside.
2. Meanwhile, heat the olive oil in a large pot or Dutch oven over medium heat. Add the chopped onion and garlic. Sauté for 5-7 minutes, or until softened and translucent.
3. Add the chopped carrots, zucchini, and celery to the pot and cook for another 5 minutes, or until slightly softened.
4. Stir in the diced tomatoes (undrained), frozen peas, dried oregano, dried thyme, and red pepper flakes (if using) to the pot. Bring to a simmer and cook for 5 minutes.
5. Add the cooked quinoa and chopped fresh spinach (or kale) to the pot. Stir gently to combine and cook for another 2-3 minutes, or until the spinach is wilted.
6. Taste the stew and adjust seasonings with salt and freshly ground black pepper (optional) as desired. Remember, the vegetable broth will contribute some sodium, so taste before adding additional salt.
7. Ladle the quinoa and vegetable stew into bowls. Garnish with chopped fresh parsley (optional) and serve hot.

NOTES
- **Quinoa alternatives:** You can substitute brown rice for the quinoa, but quinoa cooks faster and offers a complete protein source. Look for pre-cooked quinoa options labeled "low-sodium" or "no added salt" for convenience.
- **Tomato selection:** Fire-roasted tomatoes can add a smoky flavor to the stew, but any diced tomatoes will work. Opt for low-sodium canned tomatoes whenever possible.

NUTRITIONAL INFORMATION (approximate per serving):
Calories: 300 | Protein: 12g | Fat: 5g | Carbohydrates: 45g | Sodium: 350mg (depending on sodium content of ingredients) | Potassium: 500mg (depending on ingredients)

Strawberry-Blue Cheese Stream Salad with Balsamic Vinaigrette

This vibrant salad offers a delightful combination of sweet strawberries, creamy blue cheese, and a refreshing balsamic vinaigrette. Perfect for the DASH diet, this recipe focuses on low-sodium ingredients and utilizes natural sweetness from the fruit.

 **Prep Time:** 10 minutes || **Yield:** 1 serving

INGREDIENTS
For the Salad:
- 2 cups mixed greens (baby spinach, arugula, or a blend)
- ½ cup fresh strawberries, sliced
- ¼ cup crumbled blue cheese (low-sodium or regular)
- ¼ cup chopped walnuts or pecans (optional)

For the Balsamic Vinaigrette (optional):
- 2 tablespoons olive oil
- 1 tablespoon balsamic vinegar
- ½ teaspoon Dijon mustard
- Pinch of dried oregano
- Pinch of salt and freshly ground black pepper (optional)

INSTRUCTIONS
1. Wash and dry the mixed greens. Slice the fresh strawberries. Crumble the blue cheese. Chop the walnuts or pecans (optional).
2. In a large bowl, combine the mixed greens, sliced strawberries, crumbled blue cheese, and chopped walnuts or pecans (optional).
3. In a small bowl, whisk together olive oil, balsamic vinegar, Dijon mustard, dried oregano, and a pinch of salt and freshly ground black pepper (optional).
4. If using the balsamic vinaigrette, drizzle the desired amount over the salad just before serving.
5. Toss the salad gently to coat with the dressing (optional) and enjoy immediately.

NOTES
- **Vinaigrette alternatives:** If skipping the vinaigrette, you can use a squeeze of fresh lemon juice for a touch of acidity.
- **Blue cheese selection:** Opt for low-sodium blue cheese to keep sodium content in check.
- **Nut variations:** You can substitute chopped almonds or other nuts for the walnuts or pecans.
- **Leftovers:** Leftover salad components can be stored in separate airtight containers in the refrigerator. However, assembled salad is best enjoyed fresh.

NUTRITIONAL INFORMATION (approximate per serving, without vinaigrette):
Calories: 300 | Protein: 8g | Fat: 15g | Carbohydrates: 25g | Sodium: 300mg (depending on sodium content of cheese) | Potassium: 500mg (depending on ingredients)

Warm Rice and Pintos Salad with Light Vinaigrette and Fresh Herbs

This vibrant warm rice and pintos salad packed with protein-rich pinto beans and fluffy brown rice, it's tossed with a light and flavorful vinaigrette made with fresh herbs. This recipe keeps sodium content in check by using low-sodium ingredients and focusing on natural flavors.

**Prep Time:** 15 minutes || **Cook Time:** 30-35 minutes (depending on brown rice cooking time) || **Yield:** 4 servings

INGREDIENTS

For the Salad:
- 1 cup brown rice, rinsed
- 1 ½ cups low-sodium vegetable broth
- 1 (15-ounce) can pinto beans, drained and rinsed
- 1 cup chopped tomatoes (such as Roma or cherry)
- ½ cup chopped red onion
- ½ cup chopped cucumber
- ¼ cup chopped fresh cilantro
- ¼ cup chopped fresh parsley
- 2 tablespoons crumbled low-fat feta cheese (optional)

For the Light Vinaigrette:
- 2 tablespoons olive oil
- 1 tablespoon fresh lemon juice
- 1 teaspoon white wine vinegar (optional)
- ½ teaspoon dried oregano
- Pinch of garlic powder
- Pinch of freshly ground black pepper
- Salt (optional, to taste)

INSTRUCTIONS

1. In a medium saucepan, combine the rinsed brown rice and low-sodium vegetable broth. Bring to a boil, then reduce heat, cover the pan, and simmer for 30-35 minutes, or until the rice is cooked through and the liquid is absorbed.
2. In a small bowl, whisk together the olive oil, fresh lemon juice, white wine vinegar (optional), dried oregano, garlic powder, and black pepper. Season with a pinch of salt (optional) to taste.
3. While the rice cooks, prepare the other salad ingredients. In a large bowl, combine the drained and rinsed pinto beans, chopped tomatoes, chopped red onion, chopped cucumber, chopped fresh cilantro, and chopped fresh parsley.
4. Once the rice is cooked, fluff it with a fork and add it to the bowl with the other salad ingredients. Pour the light vinaigrette over the salad and toss gently to coat all ingredients evenly.
5. Transfer the warm rice and pintos salad to serving plates. Top with crumbled low-fat feta cheese (optional) for a touch of salty flavor. Serve immediately while the rice is still warm.

NOTES

- **Brown rice alternatives:** You can substitute white rice for brown rice, but brown rice offers additional fiber. Adjust the cooking time slightly for white rice.
- **Vinaigrette variations:** You can use balsamic vinegar instead of white wine vinegar for a slightly different flavor profile.

NUTRITIONAL INFORMATION (approximate per serving, without feta cheese and optional salt):

Calories: 350 | Protein: 15g | Fat: 10g | Carbohydrates: 50g | Sodium: 450mg (depending on sodium content of ingredients) | Potassium: 700mg (depending on ingredients)

Shrimp and Nectarine Salad with Lemon Herb Vinaigrette

This refreshing and flavorful salad offers a perfect light lunch or dinner option that adheres to the DASH diet. Combining juicy shrimp, sweet nectarines, and a zesty lemon herb vinaigrette, this recipe keeps sodium content in check and uses natural sweetness from the fruit for a delicious and healthy dish.

 **Prep Time:** 15 minutes || **Cook Time:** 10 minutes || **Yield:** 2 servings

INGREDIENTS
For the Salad:
- 4 ounces raw shrimp, peeled and deveined (deveining optional)
- 2 ripe nectarines, pitted and sliced
- ½ cup mixed greens (baby spinach, arugula, or a blend)
- ¼ cup crumbled low-fat feta cheese (optional)
- 2 tablespoons chopped fresh parsley

For the Lemon Herb Vinaigrette:
- 2 tablespoons olive oil
- 1 tablespoon fresh lemon juice
- 1 teaspoon Dijon mustard
- ½ teaspoon dried oregano
- Pinch of garlic powder
- Pinch of salt and freshly ground black pepper (optional)

INSTRUCTIONS
1. Heat a large skillet over medium heat. Add a drizzle of olive oil and cook the shrimp for 3-4 minutes per side, or until pink and cooked through.
2. While the shrimp cook, slice the ripe nectarines and wash and dry the mixed greens. Crumble the low-fat feta cheese (optional) and chop the fresh parsley.
3. In a large bowl, combine the mixed greens, sliced nectarines, cooked shrimp, crumbled feta cheese (optional), and chopped fresh parsley.
4. In a small bowl, whisk together olive oil, fresh lemon juice, Dijon mustard, dried oregano, garlic powder, and a pinch of salt and freshly ground black pepper (optional).
5. Drizzle the desired amount of lemon herb vinaigrette over the salad just before serving.
6. Toss the salad gently to coat with the dressing and enjoy immediately.

NOTES
- **Shrimp cooking:** Avoid overcooking the shrimp, as they can become tough.
- **Nectarine selection:** Choose ripe nectarines for the best sweetness and flavor. If not in season, you can substitute with other stone fruits like peaches or plums.
- **Feta cheese:** Crumbled low-fat feta cheese adds a salty element, but you can omit it for a completely vegan option.
- Leftovers: Leftover cooked shrimp and salad components can be stored in separate airtight containers in the refrigerator. However, assembled salad is best enjoyed fresh.

NUTRITIONAL INFORMATION (approximate per serving, without feta cheese):
Calories: 350 | Protein: 25g | Fat: 10g | Carbohydrates: 30g | Sodium: 350mg (depending on sodium content of ingredients) | Potassium: 500mg (depending on ingredients)

Green Bean Soup with Lemon and Herbs

This vibrant green bean soup is a perfect addition to the DASH diet. Packed with fresh green beans, this recipe keeps sodium content in check by using low-sodium vegetable broth and relies on fresh lemon juice and herbs for a flavorful and lightened-up soup.

 **Prep Time:** 10 minutes || **Cook Time:** 20-25 minutes || **Yield:** 4 servings

INGREDIENTS
For the Soup:
- 1 tablespoon olive oil
- 1 medium onion, chopped
- 2 cloves garlic, minced
- 1 teaspoon dried thyme
- Pinch of red pepper flakes (optional)
- 4 cups low-sodium vegetable broth
- 1 pound fresh green beans, trimmed and cut into bite-sized pieces
- 1 cup chopped carrots (optional)
- ½ cup chopped celery (optional)
- 2 tablespoons fresh lemon juice
- Salt and freshly ground black pepper (optional, to taste)
- ¼ cup chopped fresh parsley (for garnish)

INSTRUCTIONS
1. In a large pot, heat olive oil over medium heat. Add the chopped onion and cook for 3-4 minutes, or until softened. Stir in the minced garlic and dried thyme, and cook for an additional minute. Add a pinch of red pepper flakes (optional) for a touch of heat.
2. Pour in the low-sodium vegetable broth, green beans, chopped carrots (optional), and chopped celery (optional). Bring to a boil, then reduce heat and simmer for 15-20 minutes, or until the green beans and carrots are tender-crisp.
3. Stir in the fresh lemon juice and season with a pinch of salt and freshly ground black pepper (optional), to taste.
4. Ladle the hot soup into serving bowls. Garnish each bowl with a sprinkle of chopped fresh parsley.

NOTES
- **Fresh vs. frozen green beans:** Both fresh and frozen green beans work well in this recipe. If using frozen green beans, add them frozen and cook for an additional 3-5 minutes, or until heated through.
- **Herb variations:** You can substitute other fresh herbs like dill, basil, or oregano for the thyme.
- **Creamy option (not DASH-friendly):** For a richer soup, you can stir in a splash of low-fat cream or a dollop of plain Greek yogurt before serving (adds sodium).
- **Leftovers:** Leftover soup can be stored in an airtight container in the refrigerator for up to 3 days. Reheat gently on the stovetop until warmed through.

NUTRITIONAL INFORMATION (approximate per serving):
Calories: 150 | Protein: 5g | Fat: 5g | Carbohydrates: 20g | Sodium: 350mg (depending on sodium content of ingredients) | Potassium: 700mg (depending on ingredients)

Grilled Southwestern Steak Salad with Chipotle Lime Vinaigrette

This flavorful grilled southwestern steak salad offers a satisfying and protein-rich meal that perfectly fits the DASH diet. Tender grilled steak is paired with a vibrant mix of vegetables and a light and tangy chipotle lime vinaigrette, keeping sodium content in check while boasting bold Southwestern flavors.

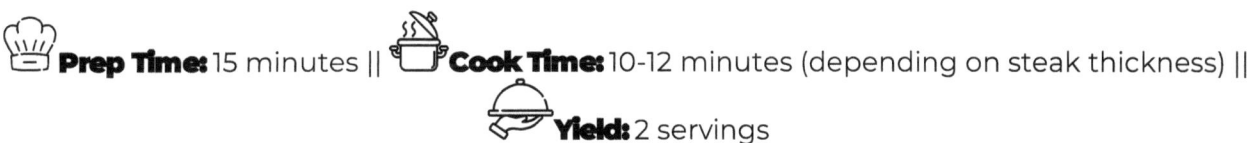

Prep Time: 15 minutes || **Cook Time:** 10-12 minutes (depending on steak thickness) || **Yield:** 2 servings

INGREDIENTS

For the Steak:
- 1 pound flank steak or skirt steak, trimmed of excess fat
- 1 tablespoon chili powder
- 1 teaspoon ground cumin
- ½ teaspoon smoked paprika
- Pinch of garlic powder
- Pinch of freshly ground black pepper
- Salt (optional, to taste)

For the Salad:
- 2 cups mixed greens (such as romaine, arugula, and spinach)
- 1 cup chopped tomatoes (such as Roma or cherry)
- ½ cup crumbled low-fat queso fresco cheese (or low-fat feta cheese)
- ½ cup chopped red onion
- ¼ cup chopped fresh cilantro
- 1 cob of corn, grilled and kernels removed (optional)
- 1 ripe avocado, sliced (optional)

For the Chipotle Lime Vinaigrette:
- 2 tablespoons olive oil
- 1 tablespoon fresh lime juice
- 1 teaspoon chopped chipotle pepper in adobo sauce (adjust to preference for spice)
- 1 teaspoon honey (or agave nectar)
- 1 clove garlic, minced
- ½ teaspoon dried oregano
- Pinch of salt (optional, to taste)

INSTRUCTIONS

1. In a shallow dish, combine the chili powder, ground cumin, smoked paprika, garlic powder, and black pepper. Rub the spice mixture onto both sides of the steak. Let the steak marinate for at least 30 minutes (or up to overnight) in the refrigerator for deeper flavor.
2. In a small bowl, whisk together the olive oil, fresh lime juice, chopped chipotle pepper in adobo sauce (adjust to your spice preference), honey (or agave nectar), minced garlic, dried oregano, and a pinch of salt (optional) to taste.
3. Preheat your grill to medium-high heat (around 400°F).
4. Season the marinated steak (if using) with a pinch of salt (optional) just before grilling. Grill the steak for 3-4 minutes per side for medium-rare, or to your desired doneness. Let the steak rest for 5 minutes before slicing thinly against the grain.
5. In a large bowl, combine the mixed greens, chopped tomatoes, crumbled queso fresco cheese (or feta cheese), chopped red onion, chopped fresh cilantro, grilled corn kernels (optional), and sliced avocado (optional).
6. Top the salad with the sliced grilled steak. Drizzle the chipotle lime vinaigrette over the salad and toss gently to coat all ingredients evenly. Serve immediately.

NOTES
- **Steak selection:** Choose a lean cut of steak like flank steak or skirt steak for this recipe.
- Grilling pan alternative: If you don't have a grill, you can cook the steak in a grill pan over medium heat on your stovetop.
- Vegetable variations: You can add other chopped vegetables to the salad, such as bell peppers, black beans, or jicama.
- Avocado variations: If omitting avocado, you can drizzle the salad with a touch of olive oil for extra richness.
- Leftovers: Leftover grilled steak can be stored in an airtight container in the refrigerator for up to 3 days. Reheat gently on the stovetop or microwave and serve over fresh salad greens with leftover vinaigrette.

NUTRITIONAL INFORMATION (approximate per serving, without optional ingredients and salt):
Calories: 450 | Protein: 40g | Fat: 20g | Carbohydrates: 30g | Sodium: 400mg (depending on sodium content of ingredients) | Potassium: 800mg (depending on ingredients)

Thai-Style Cobb Salad with Peanut Vinaigrette

This vibrant Thai-inspired cobb salad p with protein and fresh vegetables, it's dressed in a flavorful peanut vinaigrette that keeps sodium content in check while offering a burst of Asian-inspired flavors.

Prep Time: 15 minutes || **Cook Time:** 10-12 minutes (depending on chicken cooking method) || **Yield:** 2 servings

INGREDIENTS

For the Salad:
- 2 cups chopped romaine lettuce (or a mix of baby greens)
- ½ cup shredded cooked chicken breast (grilled, baked, or poached)
- ½ cup thinly sliced cucumber
- ½ cup shredded red cabbage
- ¼ cup chopped fresh cilantro
- ¼ cup chopped fresh mint (optional)
- 2 tablespoons chopped roasted peanuts (unsalted or low-sodium)

For the Peanut Vinaigrette:
- 2 tablespoons low-sodium soy sauce
- 1 tablespoon rice vinegar
- 1 tablespoon creamy peanut butter (unsweetened or low-sugar)
- 1 tablespoon freshly squeezed lime juice
- 1 tablespoon honey (or agave nectar)
- 1 clove garlic, minced
- 1 teaspoon grated ginger (optional)
- 1-2 tablespoons water (to adjust consistency)
- Pinch of red pepper flakes (optional)

INSTRUCTIONS

1. Wash and dry the romaine lettuce (or baby greens). Tear or chop the lettuce into bite-sized pieces. Shred the cooked chicken breast. Thinly slice the cucumber and shred the red cabbage. Chop the fresh cilantro and mint (optional). Toast the unsalted or low-sodium peanuts in a dry skillet over medium heat until fragrant, watching closely to avoid burning.
2. In a small bowl, whisk together the low-sodium soy sauce, rice vinegar, peanut butter, lime juice, honey (or agave nectar), minced garlic, and grated ginger (optional). Add 1 tablespoon of water and whisk until well combined. If the dressing is too thick, add another tablespoon of water to achieve a desired consistency. Season with a pinch of red pepper flakes for a touch of heat.
3. In a large bowl, combine the chopped romaine lettuce (or baby greens), shredded chicken breast, sliced cucumber, shredded red cabbage, chopped cilantro, and chopped mint (optional).
4. Drizzle the peanut vinaigrette over the salad and toss gently to coat all ingredients evenly.
5. Transfer the Thai-style cobb salad to serving plates. Sprinkle with chopped roasted peanuts for added texture and flavor. Serve immediately.

NOTES
- **Chicken alternatives:** You can use leftover grilled, baked, or poached chicken breast for this recipe. Leftover tofu, cubed and pan-fried, can be used for a vegetarian option.
- **Peanut variations:** If you have a peanut allergy, you can substitute the peanut butter in the vinaigrette with an equal amount of tahini (sesame seed paste)..

NUTRITIONAL INFORMATION (approximate per serving, without optional ingredients):
Calories: 400 | Protein: 30g | Fat: 15g | Carbohydrates: 25g | Sodium: 500mg (depending on sodium content of ingredients) | Potassium: 700mg (depending on ingredients)

PART FOUR

LUNCH & DINNER

Sesame Chicken

This flavorful and lighter take on takeout favorite sesame chicken is perfect for the DASH diet. Packed with lean protein and lower-sodium ingredients, it keeps sodium in check while still delivering delicious taste.

 **Prep Time:** 15 minutes ||  **Cook Time:** 20-25 minutes ||  **Yield:** 4 servings

INGREDIENTS
- 1 pound boneless, skinless chicken breasts, cut into bite-sized pieces
- 2 tablespoons cornstarch
- 1 tablespoon low-sodium soy sauce (or coconut aminos)
- ½ teaspoon rice vinegar
- 1 tablespoon toasted sesame oil
- 1 clove garlic, minced
- 1 teaspoon grated fresh ginger (or ½ teaspoon ground ginger)
- ½ cup low-sodium chicken broth
- 1 tablespoon water
- 1 tablespoon white sesame seeds
- 1 tablespoon chopped green onions (optional)
- Cooked broccoli florets or brown rice (for serving)

INSTRUCTIONS
1. In a medium bowl, toss the chicken pieces with cornstarch, low-sodium soy sauce (or coconut aminos), and rice vinegar. Let marinate for at least 10 minutes, or up to 30 minutes for extra flavor.
2. Heat the sesame oil in a large skillet or wok over medium heat. Add the chicken and cook for 5-7 minutes, or until golden brown and cooked through, stirring occasionally. Remove the chicken from the pan and set aside on a plate.
3. In the same pan, add the minced garlic and grated ginger. Cook for 30 seconds, stirring constantly, until fragrant.
4. In a small bowl, whisk together the low-sodium chicken broth and water. Add the broth mixture to the pan with the garlic and ginger. Bring to a simmer and scrape up any browned bits from the bottom of the pan.
5. Simmer the sauce for 1-2 minutes, or until slightly thickened.
6. Add the cooked chicken back to the pan and toss to coat with the sauce.
7. Sprinkle the white sesame seeds over the chicken and stir gently to combine. Serve the sesame chicken immediately over cooked broccoli florets or brown rice. Garnish with chopped green onions (optional).

NOTES
- **Even cooking:** To ensure the chicken cooks evenly, cut the pieces into similar sizes.
- **Sauce thickness:** You can adjust the amount of cornstarch depending on how thick you want the sauce to be. Start with 2 tablespoons and add another 1 tablespoon if you prefer a thicker consistency.
- **Low-sodium options:** Look for low-sodium soy sauce or use coconut aminos, a naturally sodium-free soy sauce substitute.

NUTRITIONAL INFORMATION (approximate per serving):
Calories: 350 | Protein: 25g | Fat: 12g (depending on oil used) | Carbohydrates: 25g | Sodium: 300mg (depending on sodium content of ingredients) | Potassium: 450mg (depending on ingredients)

Sesame Ginger Chicken with Cauliflower Rice

This flavorful sesame ginger chicken with cauliflower rice is a perfect weeknight meal option for the DASH diet. Packed with lean protein from chicken, low-carb cauliflower rice, and a delicious sauce made with low-sodium soy sauce and other DASH-friendly ingredients, it delivers a satisfying and healthy meal that keeps sodium in check.

 **Prep Time:** 15 minutes || **Cook Time:** 20-25 minutes || **Yield:** 4 servings

INGREDIENTS
For the Chicken:
 - 1 pound boneless, skinless chicken breasts, cut into bite-sized pieces
 - 2 tablespoons cornstarch
 - 1 tablespoon low-sodium soy sauce (or coconut aminos)
 - 1 tablespoon rice vinegar
 - 1 tablespoon toasted sesame oil
 - ½ teaspoon grated fresh ginger (or ½ teaspoon ground ginger)
 - 1 clove garlic, minced
 - Pinch of black pepper

For the Sesame Ginger Sauce:

 - ¼ cup low-sodium chicken broth
 - 1 tablespoon water
 - 1 tablespoon soy sauce (or coconut aminos)
 - 1 tablespoon rice vinegar
 - 1 tablespoon honey
 - 1 tablespoon toasted sesame oil
 - 1 teaspoon cornstarch
 - Pinch of garlic powder
 - Pinch of black pepper

For the Cauliflower Rice:
 - 1 head of cauliflower, cut into florets
 - 2 tablespoons water

INSTRUCTIONS
1. In a medium bowl, toss the chicken pieces with cornstarch, low-sodium soy sauce (or coconut aminos), rice vinegar, toasted sesame oil, grated ginger, minced garlic, and black pepper. Let marinate for at least 10 minutes, or up to 30 minutes for extra flavor.
2. In a food processor, pulse the cauliflower florets until they resemble rice consistency. Alternatively, you can grate the cauliflower florets using the coarse side of a box grater.
3. Heat the water in a large skillet or pan over medium heat. Add the cauliflower rice and cook for 5-7 minutes, or until tender-crisp, stirring occasionally. Season with a pinch of salt (optional) and pepper to taste.
4. In a small bowl, whisk together the low-sodium chicken broth, water, soy sauce (or coconut aminos), rice vinegar, honey, toasted sesame oil, cornstarch, garlic powder, and black pepper.
5. Heat a separate large skillet or wok over medium heat. Add a thin layer of cooking spray or a drizzle of oil and swirl to coat. Once hot, add the marinated chicken and cook for 5-7 minutes, or until golden brown and cooked through, stirring occasionally.
6. Pour the sesame ginger sauce into the pan with the cooked chicken. Bring to a simmer and cook for 1-2 minutes, or until the sauce thickens slightly.
7. Plate the cauliflower rice and top with the sesame ginger chicken. Garnish with sesame seeds (optional) and chopped green onions (optional).

NOTES
- **Low-carb option:** Cauliflower rice is a lower-carb alternative to regular rice, making this dish a great choice for the DASH diet.
- **Sodium-reduced ingredients:** Look for low-sodium soy sauce or coconut aminos to keep the sodium content in check.

- **Honey substitution:** You can substitute the honey with a touch of maple syrup or another liquid sweetener for a slightly different flavor profile.
- **Leftovers:** Leftover chicken and cauliflower rice can be stored in separate airtight containers in the refrigerator for up to 3 days. Reheat gently in a pan over low heat until warmed through.

NUTRITIONAL INFORMATION (approximate per serving):

Calories: 350 | Protein: 30g | Fat: 10g (depending on oil used) | Carbohydrates: 25g | Sodium: 400mg (depending on sodium content of ingredients) | Potassium: 500mg (depending on ingredients)

Beef and Butternut Squash Penne with Pesto

This flavorful and satisfying dish reimagines a classic beef and blue cheese pasta for the DASH diet. Packed with protein from lean beef and fiber from butternut squash, it features a lighter and lower-sodium creamy sauce made with ricotta cheese and spices, keeping sodium in check while delivering a delicious taste.

 **Prep Time:** 15 minutes || **Cook Time:** 20-25 minutes || **Yield:** 4 servings

INGREDIENTS
- 8 ounces whole-wheat penne pasta (or other whole-wheat pasta shape)
- 1 tablespoon olive oil
- 1 pound lean ground beef (90% lean or higher)
- 1 medium butternut squash, peeled and diced (about 2 cups)
- 1 clove garlic, minced
- ½ cup low-fat ricotta cheese
- ¼ cup low-sodium chicken broth
- 2 tablespoons milk (optional, for a creamier sauce)
- 1 teaspoon dried thyme
- ½ teaspoon dried rosemary
- Pinch of red pepper flakes (optional, for a touch of spice)
- Freshly ground black pepper to taste
- ¼ cup crumbled low-sodium feta cheese (or crumbled ricotta cheese for a milder option)
- ¼ cup prepared pesto (look for a low-sodium variety or make your own)
- Chopped fresh parsley (for garnish)

INSTRUCTIONS
1. Bring a large pot of salted water to a boil. Cook the whole-wheat penne pasta al dente (slightly firm to the bite). Drain the pasta and reserve about ½ cup of the cooking water.
2. In a large skillet or dutch oven, heat the olive oil over medium heat. Add the ground beef and cook, breaking it up with a spoon, until browned. Drain any excess fat.
3. Add the diced butternut squash to the pan with the cooked beef. Stir to combine and cook for 5-7 minutes, or until the squash starts to soften.
4. Add the minced garlic to the pan and cook for 30 seconds, until fragrant.
5. Stir in the low-fat ricotta cheese, low-sodium chicken broth, milk (if using), dried thyme, dried rosemary, and red pepper flakes (if using). Season with freshly ground black pepper. Bring the sauce to a simmer and cook for 2-3 minutes, or until slightly thickened. If the sauce seems too thick, add a splash or two of the reserved pasta cooking water to thin it out.
6. Add the cooked pasta and the crumbled feta cheese (or ricotta cheese) to the pan with the sauce. Toss gently to coat the pasta and cheese in the sauce. Simmer for an additional 1-2 minutes, allowing the flavors to meld.
7. Stir in the prepared pesto just before serving. Be careful not to overmix, as the pesto can lose its vibrant green color.
8. Plate the beef and butternut squash penne with pesto and garnish with chopped fresh parsley. Serve immediately.

NOTES
- **Lean ground beef:** Using lean ground beef (90% lean or higher) helps reduce saturated fat content.
- **Low-sodium feta cheese:** Look for low-sodium feta cheese to keep the sodium content in check. You can also substitute crumbled ricotta cheese for a milder flavor option.

- **Creamy sauce:** The milk is optional, and you can adjust the amount based on your desired sauce consistency.
- **Homemade pesto:** Making your own pesto allows you to control the sodium content by using low-sodium ingredients.

NUTRITIONAL INFORMATION (approximate per serving):
Calories: 500 | Protein: 30g | Fat: 20g (depending on fat content of beef) | Carbohydrates: 45g | Sodium: 500mg (depending on sodium content of ingredients) | Potassium: 700mg (depending on ingredients)

Chicken and Vegetable Penne with Parsley-Walnut Pesto

This flavorful and satisfying pasta dish is perfect for the DASH diet. Packed with protein from lean chicken and fiber-rich vegetables, it's tossed in a light and flavorful pesto made with walnuts, fresh parsley, and low-sodium ingredients. This recipe keeps sodium in check by using low-sodium alternatives and focusing on natural flavors.

Prep Time: 15 minutes || **Cook Time:** 25-30 minutes || **Yield:** 4 servings

INGREDIENTS
For the Penne and Vegetables:
 - 1 tablespoon olive oil
 - 8 ounces boneless, skinless chicken breasts, cut into bite-sized pieces
 - 1 cup chopped broccoli florets
 - ½ cup chopped bell pepper (any color)
 - 8 ounces whole-wheat penne pasta
 - Freshly ground black pepper (optional)

For the Parsley-Walnut Pesto:

 - ¾ cup chopped walnuts
 - 1 cup lightly packed fresh parsley leaves
 - 2 cloves garlic, crushed
 - ½ teaspoon dried oregano
 - Pinch of red pepper flakes (optional, for a spicy kick)
 - ¼ cup grated Parmesan cheese (optional) - see tip below
 - ⅓ cup low-sodium vegetable broth
 - 2 tablespoons olive oil

INSTRUCTIONS
1. In a large pot of boiling water, cook the whole-wheat penne usually for 8-10 minutes, or until al dente (cooked but still firm to the bite). Reserve 1 cup of the pasta cooking water before draining.
2. Meanwhile, heat the olive oil in a large skillet or pan over medium heat. Add the chopped chicken pieces and cook for 5-7 minutes, or until golden brown and cooked through. Season with freshly ground black pepper (optional) to taste.
3. Stir in the chopped broccoli florets and bell pepper. Cook for an additional 3-4 minutes, or until the vegetables are tender-crisp.
4. While the pasta cooks and the chicken and vegetables cook, prepare the pesto. In a food processor or blender, combine the chopped walnuts, fresh parsley leaves, crushed garlic, dried oregano, red pepper flakes (if using), grated Parmesan cheese (if using), low-sodium vegetable broth, and olive oil. Blend until smooth and well combined. Scrape down the sides as needed for a consistent texture.
Tip: Grated Parmesan cheese adds a savory touch, but it's higher in sodium. Use a minimal amount or omit it entirely for a strictly low-sodium option. You can substitute with a low-sodium Parmesan cheese alternative if desired.
5. Once the pasta is cooked and drained, add it to the pan with the cooked chicken and vegetables. Pour in the prepared parsley-walnut pesto and toss everything together to coat evenly. Add a splash of the reserved pasta cooking water (1-2 tablespoons) if the mixture seems too dry.
6. Divide the chicken and vegetable penne with parsley-walnut pesto among serving plates. Garnish with additional fresh parsley leaves (optional) for a touch of color. Serve hot and enjoy!

NOTES
- **Chicken options:** Skinless, boneless chicken thighs can be used instead of breasts for a more flavorful option. Adjust the cooking time slightly, as thighs take a few minutes longer to cook through.

- **Vegetable options:** Feel free to customize the vegetables based on your preferences. Other DASH-friendly options include chopped zucchini, chopped carrots, or a handful of spinach added towards the end with the broccoli.
- **Pesto leftovers:** Leftover pesto can be stored in an airtight container in the refrigerator for up to 3 days. You can use it on sandwiches, wraps, or as a dip for vegetables.

NUTRITIONAL INFORMATION (approximate per serving, without Parmesan cheese):
Calories: 450 | Protein: 30g | Fat: 20g | Carbohydrates: 40g | Sodium: 450mg (depending on sodium content of ingredients) | Potassium: 700mg (depending on ingredients)

Sheet-Pan Chicken with Roasted Spring Vegetables & Lemon Vinaigrette

This one-pan wonder is perfect for the DASH diet! Juicy chicken and colorful spring vegetables roast together, creating a flavorful and satisfying meal. The light and tangy lemon vinaigrette adds a burst of freshness without excess sodium.

 **Prep Time:** 15 minutes || **Cook Time:** 20-25 minutes || **Yield:** 4 servings

INGREDIENTS

For the Chicken and Vegetables:
- 2 (6-ounce) boneless, skinless chicken breasts
- 1 tablespoon olive oil
- ½ teaspoon dried thyme
- Pinch of garlic powder
- Freshly ground black pepper (optional)
- 1 cup asparagus spears, trimmed
- 1 cup chopped broccoli florets
- ½ cup cherry tomatoes, halved
- ½ cup sliced red onion

For the Lemon Vinaigrette:
- ¼ cup freshly squeezed lemon juice
- 2 tablespoons olive oil
- 1 tablespoon low-sodium Dijon mustard
- 1 teaspoon honey (optional, for a touch of sweetness)
- Pinch of dried oregano
- Salt and freshly ground black pepper (optional) to taste

INSTRUCTIONS

1. Preheat your oven to 425°F (220°C). Line a baking sheet with parchment paper for easier cleanup.
2. Pat the chicken breasts dry with paper towels. Season them with dried thyme, garlic powder, and freshly ground black pepper (optional) on both sides.
3. In a large bowl, toss the asparagus spears, broccoli florets, cherry tomatoes, and sliced red onion with olive oil.
4. Arrange the seasoned chicken breasts on one half of the prepared baking sheet. Spread the vegetables on the other half.
5. Bake the chicken and vegetables in the preheated oven for 20-25 minutes, or until the chicken is cooked through (internal temperature reaches 165°F) and the vegetables are tender-crisp.
6. While the chicken and vegetables roast, whisk together the freshly squeezed lemon juice, olive oil, low-sodium Dijon mustard, honey (if using), and dried oregano in a small bowl. Season with a pinch of salt and freshly ground black pepper (optional) to taste.

Tip: Taste the vinaigrette before adding additional salt, as the Dijon mustard might contribute some sodium.

7. Once cooked, carefully transfer the chicken and vegetables to serving plates. Spoon the lemon vinaigrette over the chicken and vegetables, or serve it on the side for dipping.

NOTES

- **Chicken thickness:** If your chicken breasts are thick, pound them slightly between two pieces of parchment paper to create a more even cooking surface.
- **Vegetable options:** Feel free to customize the vegetables based on your preferences. Other DASH-friendly options include chopped zucchini, chopped carrots, or a handful of sugar snap peas.

- **Leftovers:** Leftover chicken and vegetables can be stored in an airtight container in the refrigerator for up to 3 days. Reheat gently in a pan over medium heat or in the microwave until warmed through.

NUTRITIONAL INFORMATION (approximate per serving):
Calories: 400 | Protein: 35g | Fat: 15g | Carbohydrates: 30g | Sodium: 400mg (depending on sodium content of ingredients) | Potassium: 700mg (depending on ingredients)

Chicken Souvlaki with Herbed Couscous

This flavorful and satisfying dish is a perfect lightened-up version of the classic Greek souvlaki. Marinated chicken skewers are grilled or baked to juicy perfection, served alongside a bed of fluffy herbed couscous. The key to keeping it DASH-friendly lies in using low-sodium ingredients and focusing on natural flavors from herbs and spices.

Prep Time: 20 minutes (including marinating time) || **Cook Time:** 15-20 minutes (grilling) or 20-25 minutes (baking) || **Yield:** 4 servings

INGREDIENTS

For the Chicken Souvlaki:
- 1 pound boneless, skinless chicken breasts, cut into 1-inch cubes
- 1 tablespoon olive oil
- 1 tablespoon lemon juice
- ½ cup plain, non-fat Greek yogurt
- 1 teaspoon dried oregano
- ½ teaspoon dried thyme
- 1/4 teaspoon garlic powder
- Pinch of red pepper flakes (optional, for a spicy kick)
- Freshly ground black pepper (optional)
- 1 red bell pepper, cut into 1-inch pieces
- 1 red onion, cut into 1-inch pieces (optional, see tip below)

For the Herbed Couscous:
- 1 cup Israeli (pearl) couscous
- 1 ½ cups low-sodium vegetable broth
- 1 tablespoon chopped fresh parsley
- 1 tablespoon chopped fresh mint
- Pinch of dried thyme
- Salt and freshly ground black pepper (optional) to taste

INSTRUCTIONS

1. In a large bowl, combine the olive oil, lemon juice, Greek yogurt, dried oregano, dried thyme, garlic powder, red pepper flakes (if using), and freshly ground black pepper (optional). Add the chicken cubes and toss to coat them evenly in the marinade. Cover the bowl and refrigerate for at least 30 minutes, or up to 2 hours for deeper flavor.
2. While the chicken marinates, cut the red bell pepper into 1-inch pieces. You can also cut the red onion into 1-inch wedges, but for a milder onion flavor, soak the red onion wedges in a bowl of cold water for 10 minutes, then drain and pat dry before threading onto skewers.
3. If using a grill, preheat it to medium-high heat. If using the oven, preheat it to 425°F (220°C). Line a baking sheet with parchment paper for easier cleanup (baking method).
4. Thread the marinated chicken cubes and bell pepper pieces alternately onto skewers. You can use wooden or metal skewers, soaked in water for 10 minutes if using wooden skewers to prevent burning.
5. **Grilling method:** Grill the chicken skewers for 8-10 minutes per side, or until the chicken is cooked through (internal temperature reaches 165°F). **Baking method:** Bake the chicken skewers on the prepared baking sheet for 15-20 minutes per side, or until the chicken is cooked through.
6. While the chicken cooks, prepare the herbed couscous. In a saucepan, combine the Israeli couscous and low-sodium vegetable broth. Bring to a boil, then reduce heat, cover, and simmer for 15 minutes, or until the couscous is cooked through and fluffed.
7. Once cooked, remove the couscous from heat and fluff it with a fork. Stir in the chopped fresh parsley, chopped fresh mint, and dried thyme. Season with a pinch of salt and freshly ground black pepper (optional) to taste. Remember, the vegetable broth might contribute some sodium, so taste before adding additional salt.

8. Once the chicken is cooked through, remove it from the grill or oven and let it rest for a few minutes before serving. Plate the herbed couscous and top it with the chicken souvlaki skewers. Enjoy!

NOTES
- **Red onion:** Red onion adds a nice flavor to the souvlaki, but if you prefer a milder onion taste, you can omit it or soak the red onion wedges in cold water before threading them onto skewers.
- **Serving suggestions:** You can serve the chicken souvlaki and herbed couscous with a side of crumbled low-fat feta cheese (optional), a dollop of plain, non-fat Greek yogurt, or a simple salad with a light vinaigrette dressing.
- **Leftovers:** Leftover chicken souvlaki and herbed couscous can be stored in separate airtight containers in the refrigerator for up to 3 days. Reheat the chicken souvlaki gently in a pan over medium heat or in the microwave until warmed through. The couscous can be reheated in the microwave with a splash of water or low-sodium vegetable broth to prevent drying out.

NUTRITIONAL INFORMATION (approximate per serving, without feta cheese):
Calories: 400 | Protein: 30g | Fat: 10g | Carbohydrates: 40g | Sodium: 450mg (depending on sodium content of ingredients) | Potassium: 700mg (depending on ingredients)

Spinach-Stuffed Turkey Burger Patties with Avocado Crema

These juicy turkey burger patties are bursting with flavor and spinach, making them a perfect fit for the DASH diet. Lean ground turkey keeps saturated fat in check, while the spinach adds a boost of vitamins and antioxidants. The avocado crema provides a creamy and flavorful topping without excessive sodium.

**Prep Time:** 15 minutes || **Cook Time:** 15-20 minutes || **Yield:** 4 servings

INGREDIENTS

For the Turkey Burger Patties:
  - 1 pound lean ground turkey (90% lean or higher)
  - ½ cup chopped fresh spinach
  - ½ cup chopped red onion
  - 1 clove garlic, minced
  - ½ cup panko breadcrumbs (or whole wheat breadcrumbs)
  - 1 tablespoon olive oil
  - 1 tablespoon Worcestershire sauce (low-sodium)
  - 1 teaspoon dried oregano
  - ½ teaspoon dried thyme
  - Pinch of salt and freshly ground black pepper (optional)

For the Avocado Crema (optional):
  - ½ ripe avocado, mashed
  - ¼ cup low-fat Greek yogurt
  - 1 tablespoon lime juice
  - Pinch of garlic powder
  - Pinch of salt and freshly ground black pepper (optional)

For Serving (optional):
  - Whole wheat hamburger buns
  - Sliced tomato
  - Chopped lettuce
  - Red onion slices (optional)

INSTRUCTIONS

1. Preheat your grill or grill pan to medium-high heat.
2. In a large skillet, heat olive oil over medium heat. Add the chopped red onion and sauté for 2-3 minutes, or until softened. Stir in the chopped fresh spinach and cook for an additional minute, or until the spinach is wilted. Drain any excess liquid from the spinach mixture.
3. In a large bowl, combine the lean ground turkey, cooked spinach mixture, minced garlic, panko breadcrumbs, low-sodium Worcestershire sauce, dried oregano, dried thyme, and a pinch of salt and freshly ground black pepper (optional). Mix gently with your hands until just combined. Avoid overmixing.
4. Divide the turkey mixture into four equal portions. Shape each portion into a patty that's slightly wider than your hamburger buns to account for shrinking during cooking.
5. Place the burger patties on the preheated grill or grill pan. Grill for 5-7 minutes per side, or until cooked through (internal temperature reaches 165°F).
6. In a small bowl, mash together the ripe avocado, low-fat Greek yogurt, lime juice, garlic powder, and a pinch of salt and freshly ground black pepper (optional).
7. Toast the hamburger buns if desired. Place the cooked burger patties on the bottom buns. Top with sliced tomato, chopped lettuce, red onion slices (optional), and a dollop of avocado crema (optional). Enjoy!

NOTES
- **Moistness:** To prevent dry burgers, don't overmix the turkey mixture and avoid pressing down on the patties while grilling.

- **Cooking variations:** You can also bake the burger patties in a preheated oven at 400°F (200°C) for 12-15 minutes, or until cooked through.
- **Avocado crema substitutions:** If you don't have avocado, you can use low-fat sour cream or plain, non-fat Greek yogurt as a substitute.
- **Leftovers:** Leftover cooked burger patties can be stored in an airtight container in the refrigerator for up to 3 days. Reheat gently on the stovetop or in the microwave until warmed through.

NUTRITIONAL INFORMATION (approximate per serving, without avocado crema):
Calories: 400 | Protein: 30g | Fat: 15g | Carbohydrates: 30g | Sodium: 450mg (depending on sodium content of ingredients) | Potassium: 500mg (depending on ingredients)

Turkey Medallions with Herb-Marinated Tomato Salad

This recipe takes inspiration from the classic turkey medallions with tomato salad, but with adjustments to make it more DASH-friendly. Here, we focus on using low-sodium ingredients and flavorful herbs for a satisfying and nutritious meal.

Prep Time: 15 minutes || **Cook Time:** 15-20 minutes || **Yield:** 4 servings

INGREDIENTS

For the Turkey Medallions:
- 1 pound boneless, skinless turkey breast cutlets, sliced into thin medallions
- 2 tablespoons olive oil
- 1 tablespoon dried Italian seasoning
- ½ teaspoon dried thyme
- Pinch of freshly ground black pepper

For the Herb-Marinated Tomato Salad:
- 2 large tomatoes, sliced
- 1 cucumber, thinly sliced
- ½ red onion, thinly sliced
- ¼ cup crumbled low-fat feta cheese (optional)
- ¼ cup chopped fresh parsley
- 2 tablespoons olive oil
- 1 tablespoon balsamic vinegar
- ½ teaspoon dried oregano
- Pinch of salt and freshly ground black pepper (optional)

INSTRUCTIONS

1. In a large bowl, combine olive oil, dried Italian seasoning, dried thyme, and a pinch of freshly ground black pepper. Add the turkey medallions and toss to coat them evenly in the marinade. Let the turkey marinate for at least 15 minutes, or up to 30 minutes for deeper flavor.
2. While the turkey marinates, combine the sliced tomatoes, cucumber, red onion, crumbled low-fat feta cheese (optional), and chopped fresh parsley in a large bowl.
3. In a small bowl, whisk together olive oil, balsamic vinegar, dried oregano, and a pinch of salt and freshly ground black pepper (optional).
4. Heat a large skillet over medium heat. Add the marinated turkey medallions and cook for 5-7 minutes per side, or until cooked through (internal temperature reaches 165°F).
5. Divide the herb-marinated tomato salad among serving plates. Top each plate with cooked turkey medallions. Drizzle with any remaining marinade from the salad for extra flavor. Enjoy immediately!

NOTES

- **Pounding the turkey:** Pounding the turkey medallions to a thinner, even thickness can help ensure even cooking.
- **Herb variations:** Experiment with different fresh herbs like rosemary, thyme, or basil for a variety of flavors in the marinade.
- **Feta cheese:** Crumbled low-fat feta cheese adds a salty element, but you can omit it for a completely vegetarian option.
- **Leftovers:** Leftover cooked turkey medallions and tomato salad can be stored in separate airtight containers in the refrigerator for up to 3 days. Reheat the turkey gently on the stovetop or in the microwave until warmed through.

NUTRITIONAL INFORMATION (approximate per serving, without feta cheese):
Calories: 350 | Protein: 30g | Fat: 15g | Carbohydrates: 20g | Sodium: 400mg (depending on sodium content of ingredients) | Potassium: 700mg (depending on ingredients)

Creamy Lemon Pasta with Shrimp

This light and flavorful creamy lemon pasta with shrimp is a delicious and satisfying meal option for the DASH diet. Packed with protein from the shrimp and whole-wheat pasta, and a sauce made with low-sodium alternatives, it keeps sodium in check while delivering a taste sensation.

Prep Time: 15 minutes || **Cook Time:** 15-20 minutes || **Yield:** 4 servings

INGREDIENTS

- 8 ounces whole-wheat penne pasta (or other whole-wheat pasta shape)
- 1 tablespoon olive oil
- 1 clove garlic, minced
- 1 pound raw, peeled and deveined shrimp (thawed and patted dry)
- ½ cup low-fat ricotta cheese
- ¼ cup fat-free plain Greek yogurt
- ¼ cup grated Parmesan cheese (optional)
- ¼ cup low-sodium chicken broth
- 2 tablespoons lemon juice
- 1 teaspoon dried parsley
- Pinch of red pepper flakes (optional, for a touch of spice)
- Freshly ground black pepper to taste
- Chopped fresh parsley (for garnish)

INSTRUCTIONS

1. Bring a large pot of salted water to a boil. Cook the whole-wheat penne pasta al dente (slightly firm to the bite). Drain the pasta, reserving about ½ cup of the cooking water.
2. While the pasta is cooking, heat the olive oil in a large skillet or pan over medium heat. Add the minced garlic and cook for 30 seconds, until fragrant. Add the shrimp and cook for 2-3 minutes per side, or until pink and cooked through. Remove the shrimp from the pan and set aside on a plate.
3. In the same pan used to cook the shrimp, whisk together the low-fat ricotta cheese, fat-free plain Greek yogurt, Parmesan cheese (if using), low-sodium chicken broth, lemon juice, dried parsley, and red pepper flakes (if using). Season with freshly ground black pepper.
4. Bring the sauce to a simmer over medium heat, whisking constantly. Simmer for 2-3 minutes, or until slightly thickened. If the sauce seems too thick, add a splash or two of the reserved pasta cooking water to thin it out.
5. Add the cooked pasta and shrimp back to the pan with the sauce. Toss gently to coat the pasta and shrimp in the creamy lemon sauce.
6. Plate the creamy lemon pasta with shrimp and garnish with chopped fresh parsley. Serve immediately.

NOTES

- **Low-fat options:** Using low-fat ricotta cheese and fat-free plain Greek yogurt helps keep the sodium and fat content in check.
- **Parmesan cheese:** Parmesan cheese adds a savory flavor, but it's higher in sodium. You can omit it entirely or use a small amount and sprinkle it on top of each serving for a touch of flavor without adding too much sodium.
- **Fresh herbs:** Chopped fresh dill can be a great substitute for dried parsley in the sauce.

NUTRITIONAL INFORMATION (approximate per serving, without Parmesan cheese):

Calories: 400 | Protein: 30g | Fat: 15g | Carbohydrates: 40g | Sodium: 400mg (depending on sodium content of ingredients) | Potassium: 500mg (depending on ingredients)

Middle Eastern Hummus Wrap with Whole Wheat Pita and Roasted Vegetables

This colorful wrap offers a flavorful and satisfying lunch or light dinner option that fits perfectly into the DASH diet. Packed with protein and fiber from the hummus and vegetables, this recipe keeps sodium in check by using low-sodium ingredients and focusing on natural flavors.

Prep Time: 15 minutes || **Cook Time:** 30-35 minutes (depending on roasting time) || **Yield:** 2 wraps

INGREDIENTS
For the Roasted Vegetables:
- 1 tablespoon olive oil
- 1 cup chopped bell peppers (red, yellow, or orange)
- ½ cup chopped zucchini
- ½ cup chopped broccoli florets
- Pinch of dried oregano
- Pinch of salt and freshly ground black pepper (optional)

For the Wraps:
- 2 whole wheat pita breads
- ½ cup hummus (low-sodium or homemade)
- ¼ cup crumbled low-fat feta cheese (optional)
- ½ cup chopped cucumber
- ¼ cup chopped red onion (optional)
- ¼ cup chopped fresh parsley
- Pinch of dried oregano (optional)
- Extra virgin olive oil (for drizzling, optional)

INSTRUCTIONS
1. Preheat your oven to 400°F (200°C).
2. In a bowl, toss the chopped bell peppers, zucchini, and broccoli florets with olive oil, dried oregano, and a pinch of salt and freshly ground black pepper (optional).
3. Spread the vegetables on a baking sheet and roast in the preheated oven for 20-25 minutes, or until tender-crisp.
4. While the vegetables roast, you can warm the whole wheat pita breads in a toaster oven or skillet over medium heat for a few seconds per side, until slightly softened and warmed through.
5. Spread a layer of hummus (low-sodium or homemade) on each warmed pita bread. Top with half of the roasted vegetables, crumbled low-fat feta cheese (optional), chopped cucumber, chopped red onion (optional), and chopped fresh parsley. Sprinkle with a pinch of dried oregano (optional) for extra flavor. Drizzle with a touch of extra virgin olive oil for an extra flavor boost (optional).
6. Fold the bottom of the pita bread up and over the filling, then fold the sides in to create a wrap.

NOTES
- **Roasting vegetables:** You can add other vegetables to the roasting pan, such as chopped carrots, cherry tomatoes, or eggplant. Adjust roasting time based on the chosen vegetables.
- **Feta cheese:** Crumbled low-fat feta cheese adds a salty element, but you can omit it for a completely vegan option.

NUTRITIONAL INFORMATION (approximate per serving, without feta cheese):
Calories: 400 | Protein: 10g | Fat: 15g | Carbohydrates: 50g | Sodium: 400mg (depending on sodium content of ingredients) | Potassium: 700mg (depending on ingredients)

Lemon-Garlic Shrimp Over Orzo with Zucchini

This light and flavorful dish is a perfect example of a DASH-friendly recipe. It combines succulent shrimp, protein-rich orzo, and zucchini for a satisfying and nutritious meal. The dish is bursting with lemon-garlic flavor, and keeps sodium content in check.

 **Prep Time:** 10 minutes || **Cook Time:** 20 minutes || **Yield:** 4 servings

INGREDIENTS
- 1 ½ pounds fresh or frozen (thawed and patted dry) large shrimp, peeled and deveined
- 2 tablespoons olive oil
- 3 cloves garlic, minced
- 1 lemon, zested and juiced
- ¼ teaspoon dried oregano
- Pinch of red pepper flakes (optional)
- ¼ cup dry white wine (optional)
- ¾ cup dried orzo pasta
- 2 cups sliced zucchini
- ¼ cup chopped fresh parsley
- Salt and freshly ground black pepper to taste

INSTRUCTIONS
1. In a large bowl, toss the shrimp with 1 tablespoon of olive oil, lemon zest, oregano, and red pepper flakes (if using). Season with a pinch of salt and pepper. Set aside to marinate for 10 minutes (optional, but recommended for added flavor).
2. Heat the remaining 1 tablespoon of olive oil in a large skillet over medium heat. Add the garlic and cook for 30 seconds, until fragrant. Be careful not to burn the garlic.
3. Add the shrimp to the pan and cook for 3-4 minutes per side, or until opaque and cooked through. Remove the shrimp from the pan and set aside in a warm place.
4. If using white wine, deglaze the pan by pouring in the wine and scraping up any browned bits from the bottom. Let the wine simmer for a minute or two to reduce slightly.
5. Add the orzo pasta and 2 cups of water to the pan. Bring to a boil, then reduce heat and simmer, or until the orzo is al dente (cooked but still firm to the bite).
6. While the orzo cooks, add the sliced zucchini to the pan along with a splash of water or broth to prevent sticking. Cook for 3-4 minutes, or until the zucchini is tender-crisp.
7. Once the orzo is cooked, stir in the cooked shrimp, lemon juice, and chopped parsley. Season with salt and pepper to taste.
8. Serve the lemon-garlic shrimp over the orzo and zucchini mixture.

NOTES
- If you don't have white wine, you can substitute with chicken broth.
- Adjust the amount of red pepper flakes to your spice preference.
- For a vegetarian option, omit the shrimp and add another cup of cooked chickpeas or lentils for extra protein.
- Serve with a side of steamed broccoli or a green salad for a complete and balanced meal.

NUTRITIONAL INFORMATION (approximate per serving):
Calories: 400 | Protein: 30g | Fat: 15g | Carbohydrates: 35g | Sodium: 350mg (depending on sodium content of ingredients) | Potassium: 500mg (depending on ingredients)

Fresh Shrimp Spring Rolls with Peanut Dipping Sauce

These fresh shrimp spring rolls are a vibrant and flavorful appetizer or light lunch option perfect for the DASH diet. Packed with protein from shrimp, fresh and colorful vegetables, and wrapped in whole-wheat rice paper, they deliver a satisfying and healthy meal that keeps sodium in check.

**Prep Time:** 15 minutes || **Cook Time:** No cook || **Yield:** 4-6 spring rolls

INGREDIENTS
For the Spring Rolls:
- 8 sheets whole-wheat rice paper (10-inch diameter)
- 1 pound cooked, deveined, and peeled shrimp (medium or large)
- 1 cup shredded carrots
- ½ cup chopped cucumber
- ½ cup shredded red cabbage (or lettuce leaves)
- ½ cup chopped fresh bean sprouts
- ¼ cup chopped fresh mint
- ¼ cup chopped fresh cilantro
- 1 tablespoon chopped fresh basil (optional)

For the Peanut Dipping Sauce (Low-Sodium Option):
- ¼ cup unsalted creamy peanut butter
- ¼ cup low-sodium soy sauce (or coconut aminos)
- 2 tablespoons rice vinegar
- 1 tablespoon water
- 1 tablespoon honey or maple syrup (optional)
- 1 teaspoon sriracha sauce (optional, adjust for spice preference)
- 1 clove garlic, minced
- 1 tablespoon lime juice
- Pinch of ground ginger

INSTRUCTIONS
1. Fill a large, shallow bowl with warm water. This will be used to soften the rice paper wrappers.
2. Shred the carrots, chop the cucumber, and shred the red cabbage (or lettuce). Wash and pat dry the fresh herbs (mint, cilantro, and basil, if using).
3. Have all your ingredients and a clean work surface prepared. Dip one rice paper wrapper into the warm water for a few seconds, just until softened and pliable. Carefully lay it flat on a plate or cutting board.
4. Arrange a few shrimp, some shredded carrots, chopped cucumber, red cabbage (or lettuce), bean sprouts, and fresh herbs in the center of the softened rice paper wrapper.
5. Fold the bottom of the rice paper wrapper over the filling. Then, fold in the sides tightly. Gently but firmly roll up the spring roll, like a burrito. Repeat with the remaining rice paper wrappers and filling ingredients.
6. In a small bowl, whisk together the unsalted creamy peanut butter, low-sodium soy sauce (or coconut aminos), rice vinegar, water, honey or maple syrup (if using), sriracha sauce (if using), minced garlic, lime juice, and ground ginger. Taste and adjust seasonings as desired. The sauce should be creamy with a balance of sweet, savory, and slightly spicy flavors.
7. Serve the fresh shrimp spring rolls with the peanut dipping sauce on the side. Enjoy them fresh for the best texture and flavor.

NOTES
- **Cooking the shrimp:** You can boil, poach, grill, or bake the shrimp according to your preference. Just make sure they are cooked through and cooled before using.
- **Rice paper selection:** Look for whole-wheat rice paper wrappers for added fiber content.
- **Vegetable options:** Feel free to customize the vegetables based on your preferences. Other DASH-friendly options include shredded bell peppers, chopped spinach, or shredded zucchini.

- **Peanut butter selection:** Choose a natural creamy peanut butter with no added sugar or salt for a lower-sodium option.
- **Leftovers:** Leftover spring rolls can be stored in an airtight container in the refrigerator for up to 2 hours. The rice paper wrappers might become slightly tough, but they are still enjoyable. The dipping sauce can be stored in a separate container in the refrigerator for up to 3 days.

NUTRITIONAL INFORMATION (approximate per serving, without dipping sauce):
Calories: 250 | Protein: 20g | Fat: 5g | Carbohydrates: 25g | Sodium: 200mg (depending on sodium content of ingredients) | Potassium: 400mg (depending on ingredients)

Walnut-Rosemary Crusted Salmon

This delicious and easy walnut-crusted salmon is a perfect DASH-friendly main course. Packed with omega-3 fatty acids from the salmon and healthy fats from the walnuts, it features a flavorful and satisfying crust made with herbs and spices. This recipe keeps sodium in check by using low-sodium alternatives and focusing on natural flavors.

 **Prep Time:** 15 minutes || **Cook Time:** 10-12 minutes || **Yield:** 2 servings

INGREDIENTS

For the Salmon:
- 2 (6-ounce) skinless salmon fillets
- 1 tablespoon olive oil
- Freshly ground black pepper (optional)

For the Walnut-Rosemary Crust:
- ½ cup chopped walnuts
- 2 tablespoons whole-wheat breadcrumbs
- 1 tablespoon grated Parmesan cheese (optional)
- 1 teaspoon chopped fresh rosemary
- ½ teaspoon dried thyme
- Pinch of garlic powder
- Pinch of red pepper flakes (optional, for a spicy kick)

INSTRUCTIONS

1. Preheat your oven to 425°F (220°C). Lightly grease a baking sheet or line it with parchment paper for easier cleanup.
2. Pat the salmon fillets dry with paper towels. Season them lightly with freshly ground black pepper (optional) on both sides.
3. In a food processor or blender, combine the chopped walnuts, whole-wheat breadcrumbs, grated Parmesan cheese (if using), chopped fresh rosemary, dried thyme, garlic powder, and red pepper flakes (if using). Pulse a few times until the mixture resembles a coarse crumble.
4. Place the salmon fillets on the prepared baking sheet. Spread the walnut-rosemary crust evenly over the top of each salmon fillet, pressing gently to adhere.
5. Bake the salmon fillets in the preheated oven for 10-12 minutes, or until the salmon is cooked through and flakes easily with a fork. The internal temperature of the salmon should reach 145°F (63°C) for safe consumption.
6. Once cooked, carefully transfer the salmon fillets to serving plates. Enjoy them immediately with your favorite DASH-friendly side dishes, such as roasted vegetables, quinoa salad, or brown rice.

NOTES

- **Parmesan cheese:** Grated Parmesan cheese adds a savory touch, but it's higher in sodium. Use a minimal amount or omit it entirely for a strictly low-sodium option. You can substitute with a low-sodium Parmesan cheese alternative if desired.
- **Breadcrumbs:** Whole-wheat breadcrumbs offer a fiber boost compared to regular breadcrumbs. You can also use panko breadcrumbs for a lighter and crispier crust, but be aware that they might be slightly higher in sodium. Opt for low-sodium panko if available.

NUTRITIONAL INFORMATION (approximate per serving, without Parmesan cheese):
Calories: 400 | Protein: 30g | Fat: 20g | Carbohydrates: 20g | Sodium: 300mg (depending on sodium content of ingredients) | Potassium: 700mg (depending on ingredients)

Lemon-Herb Salmon with Caponata and Farro

This recipe takes inspiration from the classic lemon-herb salmon with caponata and farro, but with adjustments to make it more DASH-friendly. Focusing on low-sodium ingredients and natural flavors, this dish offers a delicious and nutritious option that fits the DASH diet.

 **Prep Time:** 15 minutes || **Cook Time:** 40-45 minutes || **Yield:** 4 servings

INGREDIENTS

For the Caponata:
- 1 tablespoon olive oil
- 1 medium eggplant, diced (about 1 cup)
- 1 red bell pepper, diced (about 1 cup)
- 1 celery stalk, diced (optional)
- ½ cup chopped red onion
- 2 cloves garlic, minced
- 1 (14.5-ounce) can diced tomatoes, undrained (fire-roasted or seasoned, for added flavor)
- ¼ cup chopped fresh parsley
- 2 tablespoons balsamic vinegar
- ½ teaspoon dried oregano
- Pinch of red pepper flakes (optional)
- Salt and freshly ground black pepper (optional) to taste

For the Farro:
- ⅔ cup farro
- 1 ½ cups low-sodium vegetable broth

For the Salmon:
- 4 (4-ounce) salmon fillets (skin-on or skinless)
- 1 tablespoon olive oil
- 1 teaspoon lemon zest
- ½ teaspoon dried thyme
- Pinch of dried rosemary
- Salt and freshly ground black pepper (optional) to taste
- Lemon wedges (for serving)

INSTRUCTIONS

1. Preheat your oven to 400°F (200°C).
2. In a large skillet, heat olive oil over medium heat. Add the diced eggplant, red bell pepper, celery stalk (optional), and red onion. Sauté for 5-7 minutes, or until the vegetables are softened.
3. Stir in the minced garlic, diced tomatoes (undrained), chopped fresh parsley, balsamic vinegar, dried oregano, and red pepper flakes (optional). Bring to a simmer and cook for an additional 5 minutes, or until the flavors meld. Season with a pinch of salt and freshly ground black pepper (optional) to taste. Remove the caponata from the heat and set aside.
4. In a saucepan, combine the farro and low-sodium vegetable broth. Bring to a boil, then reduce heat to low, cover, and simmer for about 30 minutes, or until the farro is tender and fluffy. Fluff the farro with a fork and set aside.
5. Pat the salmon fillets dry with paper towels. In a small bowl, combine olive oil, lemon zest, dried thyme, dried rosemary, salt, and freshly ground black pepper (optional) to taste. Rub the salmon fillets with the herb mixture.
6. Place the seasoned salmon fillets on a baking sheet lined with parchment paper. Bake for 15-20 minutes, or until the salmon is cooked through (flaky when tested with a fork).
7. Divide the cooked farro among serving plates. Top with the warmed caponata and a baked salmon fillet. Garnish with lemon wedges and serve immediately.

NOTES
- **Low-sodium capers:** If you typically enjoy capers in your caponata, consider using a low-sodium variety to keep the sodium content in check.

- **Salmon skin:** You can bake the salmon with the skin on or remove it before baking. If leaving the skin on, score the skin with a sharp knife to prevent curling during cooking.
- **Leftovers:** Leftover salmon, caponata, and farro can be stored in separate airtight containers in the refrigerator for up to 3 days. Reheat gently on the stovetop or in the microwave until warmed through.

NUTRITIONAL INFORMATION (approximate per serving):
Calories: 450 | Protein: 30g | Fat: 15g | Carbohydrates: 40g | Sodium: 500mg (depending on sodium content of ingredients) | Potassium: 800mg (depending on ingredients)

Sweet Potato and Black Bean Tacos

These flavorful tacos fits perfectly with the DASH diet. The roasted sweet potatoes provide natural sweetness and fiber, while the black beans offer a protein punch. This recipe keeps sodium in check with low-sodium ingredients and flavorful spices.

 **Prep Time:** 10 minutes || **Cook Time:** 40-45 minutes || **Yield:** 4 servings

INGREDIENTS

- 1 large sweet potato, peeled and diced into 1-inch cubes
- 1 tablespoon olive oil
- ½ teaspoon smoked paprika
- ¼ teaspoon ground cumin
- Pinch of cayenne pepper (optional)
- 1 (15 oz) can low-sodium black beans, rinsed and drained
- 1 cup chopped tomatoes (fresh or canned, diced)
- ½ cup chopped red onion
- ¼ cup chopped fresh cilantro
- 2 tablespoons lime juice
- 1 tablespoon chopped fresh jalapeno (optional)
- 4 corn tortillas (whole wheat or white) warmed
- Toppings (optional):
  - Chopped avocado
  - Low-fat crumbled queso fresco cheese
  - Diced red onion
  - Fresh cilantro sprigs
  - Low-fat sour cream (optional)

INSTRUCTIONS

1. Preheat oven to 400°F (200°C). Line a baking sheet with parchment paper.
2. Toss the diced sweet potato cubes with olive oil, smoked paprika, cumin, and cayenne pepper (if using). Spread the sweet potatoes in a single layer on the prepared baking sheet.
3. Roast the sweet potatoes for 25-30 minutes, or until tender and slightly browned, flipping halfway through.
4. While the sweet potatoes are roasting, prepare the black bean mixture. In a medium skillet, heat a drizzle of olive oil over medium heat. Add the chopped red onion and cook for 2-3 minutes, until softened.
5. Add the drained black beans, chopped tomatoes, lime juice, and chopped jalapeno (if using) to the skillet. Season with salt and pepper to taste (start with a small amount of salt, as black beans can be salty). Heat through for a few minutes, stirring occasionally.
6. Warm the corn tortillas (microwave, stovetop, or oven).
7. To assemble the tacos, spoon the roasted sweet potatoes onto the warmed tortillas. Top with the black bean mixture, chopped avocado (optional), queso fresco cheese (optional), diced red onion, fresh cilantro sprigs, and a dollop of low-fat sour cream (optional).

NOTES

- If you don't have fresh jalapeno, you can substitute with a pinch of red pepper flakes for a touch of heat.
- You can also use a pre-cooked rotisserie chicken breast, shredded, for added protein.
- For a vegan option, omit the cheese and sour cream and add a plant-based yogurt drizzle instead.

NUTRITIONAL INFORMATION (approximate per serving, without optional toppings):
Calories: 350 | Protein: 10g | Fat: 10g | Carbohydrates: 45g | Sodium: 400mg (depending on sodium content of ingredients) | Potassium: 700mg (depending on ingredients)

Southwest Tofu Scramble

This protein-packed scramble is a delicious and heart-healthy breakfast option perfect for the DASH diet. It's loaded with vegetables, low in sodium, and bursting with Southwestern flavors.

Prep Time: 10 minutes || **Cook Time:** 15 minutes || **Yield:** 2 servings

INGREDIENTS

- 1 tablespoon olive oil
- 1 block (14 oz) extra-firm tofu, drained and pressed
- ½ cup chopped bell pepper (any color)
- ½ cup chopped onion
- 1 clove garlic, minced
- ½ cup chopped green chiles (optional, adjust for spice preference)
- ½ cup diced tomatoes (fresh or canned, drained)
- ½ cup canned black beans, rinsed and drained
- 1 teaspoon chili powder
- ½ teaspoon smoked paprika
- ¼ teaspoon cumin
- ¼ teaspoon dried oregano
- Pinch of cayenne pepper (optional)
- Salt and freshly ground black pepper to taste
- ¼ cup chopped fresh cilantro
- 2 tablespoons crumbled low-fat feta cheese (optional)
- ¼ cup chopped avocado (optional)

INSTRUCTIONS

1. Heat olive oil in a large skillet over medium heat. Crumble the tofu with your hands or a fork into bite-sized pieces. Add the crumbled tofu to the pan and cook for 5-7 minutes, stirring occasionally, until lightly golden brown.
2. Add the bell pepper, onion, and garlic to the pan. Cook for 5 minutes, or until softened and translucent. Stir in the green chiles (if using).
3. Add the diced tomatoes, black beans, chili powder, paprika, cumin, oregano, and cayenne pepper (if using). Season with salt and pepper to taste. Cook for an additional 2-3 minutes, or until heated through.
4. Remove from heat and stir in the fresh cilantro.
5. Divide the scramble between two plates. Top with crumbled feta cheese (optional) and chopped avocado (optional) for extra flavor and creaminess.

NOTES

- To press the tofu, wrap it in a clean kitchen towel and place a heavy object (like a cutting board or a pot) on top for 15-20 minutes. This helps remove excess moisture for a better texture.
- Use low-sodium canned diced tomatoes or black beans to keep the sodium content in check.
- Adjust the spices to your taste preference. You can add a pinch of red pepper flakes for extra heat.
- For a vegan option, omit the feta cheese.
- Serve with a side of whole-wheat toast or a whole-wheat tortilla for a complete and satisfying breakfast.

NUTRITIONAL INFORMATION (approximate per serving, without optional toppings):

Calories: 300 | Protein: 20g | Fat: 10g | Carbohydrates: 30g | Sodium: 400mg (depending on sodium content of ingredients) | Potassium: 500mg (depending on ingredients)

Mediterranean Quinoa Bowls with Roasted Red Pepper Sauce

This vibrant and flavorful dish is a perfect example of a delicious and satisfying meal that fits perfectly with the DASH diet. Packed with protein, fiber, and healthy fats, it's bursting with Mediterranean flavors while keeping sodium in check.

Prep Time: 15 minutes || **Cook Time:** (depending on cook time for quinoa and roasting time for peppers) || **Yield:** 4 servings

INGREDIENTS
For the Roasted Red Pepper Sauce:
- 2 red bell peppers, halved and seeded
- 1 clove garlic, minced
- 1/2 cup low-sodium vegetable broth
- 1 tablespoon olive oil
- 1 tablespoon lemon juice
- Pinch of dried oregano
- Pinch of red pepper flakes (optional)
- Salt and freshly ground black pepper to taste

For the Mediterranean Quinoa Bowls:

- 1 cup rinsed quinoa
- 1 ½ cups low-sodium vegetable broth
- 1 cucumber, diced
- ½ cup crumbled feta cheese (optional, for a vegetarian option use crumbled tofu)
- ¼ cup Kalamata olives, pitted and halved
- ¼ cup chopped red onion
- 1 handful cherry tomatoes, halved
- ¼ cup chopped fresh parsley
- Extra virgin olive oil, lemon juice, salt, and pepper for drizzling (to taste)

INSTRUCTIONS
1. Preheat oven to 400°F (200°C). Line a baking sheet with parchment paper. Place the halved red bell peppers, cut side down, on the prepared baking sheet. Roast for 20-25 minutes, or until softened and blistered.
   - Once roasted, remove the peppers from the oven and place them in a plastic bag to steam for 10 minutes. This will loosen the skins.
   - After steaming, peel off the skins from the peppers (discard) and roughly chop the flesh.
   - In a blender or food processor, combine the chopped roasted peppers, garlic, vegetable broth, olive oil, lemon juice, oregano, and red pepper flakes (if using). Blend until smooth. Season with salt and pepper to taste. Set aside.
2. In a medium saucepan, combine the rinsed quinoa and vegetable broth. Bring to a boil, then reduce heat, cover, and simmer for 15-20 minutes, or until the quinoa is cooked through and fluffy.
3. Divide the cooked quinoa among 4 bowls.
   - Top each bowl with diced cucumber, crumbled feta cheese (or tofu for vegetarian option), Kalamata olives, chopped red onion, cherry tomato halves, and chopped fresh parsley.
   - Drizzle each bowl with a generous amount of the roasted red pepper sauce.
   - Finish with a drizzle of extra virgin olive oil, lemon juice, and a sprinkle of salt and pepper to taste (optional).

NOTES
- You can roast the red peppers on a stovetop grill pan over medium heat for a smoky flavor. Blister the skin on all sides, then transfer the peppers to a paper bag to steam and remove the skins.

- For a thicker sauce, remove some of the roasted pepper flesh before blending and add it back in after blending for a chunky texture.
- If you don't have fresh parsley, you can substitute with 1 teaspoon of dried parsley.
- Leftovers can be stored in an airtight container in the refrigerator for up to 3 days. Reheat gently before serving.

NUTRITIONAL INFORMATION (approximate per serving, without optional feta cheese):
Calories: 400 | Protein: 12g (with feta) or 8g (with tofu) | Fat: 15g | Carbohydrates: 50g | Sodium: 350mg (depending on sodium content of ingredients) | Potassium: 500mg (depending on ingredients)

Veggie and Hummus Sandwich

This colorful and satisfying veggie and hummus sandwich is a perfect lunch option for the DASH diet. Packed with fiber-rich whole-wheat bread, protein from chickpeas in the hummus, and a variety of fresh vegetables, it delivers deliciousness while keeping sodium in check.

 **Prep Time:** 5 minutes || **Cook Time:** No cook || **Yield:** 1 serving

INGREDIENTS
- 2 slices whole-wheat bread
- 3 tablespoons hummus (choose a low-sodium variety)
- ¼ cup mixed salad greens
- ¼ medium cucumber, sliced
- ¼ medium red bell pepper, sliced
- ¼ cup shredded carrots
- 2-3 slices avocado (optional)
- Sprouts (alfalfa or broccoli, optional)
- Salt and pepper to taste

INSTRUCTIONS
1. Spread 1 to 1 ½ tablespoons of hummus on each slice of whole-wheat bread.
2. Layer your favorite vegetables on one slice of bread. Start with the mixed salad greens for a base, followed by cucumber slices, red bell pepper slices, and shredded carrots.
3. If using avocado, add a few slices on top of the other vegetables.
4. Sprinkle some sprouts on top of the vegetables for added crunch and nutrition.
5. Season with a pinch of salt and pepper to taste. Top the sandwich with the other slice of bread spread with hummus.
6. Cut the sandwich in half (diagonally for a more visually appealing presentation, optional) and enjoy!

NOTES
- **Hummus variety:** Choose a low-sodium variety of hummus or make your own to control the sodium content.
- **Vegetable options:** Feel free to customize the vegetables based on your preferences. Other DASH-friendly options include sliced tomatoes, chopped spinach, or roasted vegetables.
- **Creamy texture:** For a creamier spread, mash half an avocado and mix it with the hummus before spreading it on the bread.
- **Portion control:** Be mindful of portion sizes, especially with the hummus, as it can be higher in calories.
- **Leftovers:** While not ideal, leftover halves can be wrapped tightly and stored in the refrigerator for up to 2 hours. The vegetables might lose some crispness, but the sandwich can still be enjoyed.

Veggie Quesadillas with Cilantro Yogurt Dip

These veggie quesadillas with a flavorful cilantro yogurt dip are a perfect light lunch or satisfying vegetarian dinner option for the DASH diet. Packed with fiber-rich vegetables and whole-wheat tortillas, along with a protein and calcium-rich yogurt dip, they deliver a delicious and balanced meal that keeps sodium in check.

 **Prep Time:** 10 minutes || **Cook Time:** 15-20 minutes || **Yield:** 4 servings

INGREDIENTS

For the Quesadillas:
- 12 (6-inch) whole-wheat tortillas
- 1 ½ cups shredded low-fat mozzarella cheese
- 1 cup chopped bell peppers (mix of colors)
- ½ cup chopped zucchini
- ½ cup chopped mushrooms (optional)
- ½ cup chopped black beans (canned or cooked)
- ¼ cup chopped fresh cilantro
- Pinch of chili powder (optional)
- Pinch of ground cumin (optional)
- Cooking spray

For the Cilantro Yogurt Dip:
- 2 cups plain, non-fat Greek yogurt
- ¼ cup chopped fresh cilantro
- ½ teaspoon lime juice
- Pinch of garlic powder
- Pinch of black pepper

INSTRUCTIONS

1. Chop the bell peppers, zucchini, and mushrooms (if using) into small pieces.
2. Heat a large skillet or griddle over medium heat. Coat the pan with cooking spray.
3. Place one whole-wheat tortilla on the preheated skillet. Sprinkle with ¼ cup of shredded mozzarella cheese. Top with a layer of the chopped vegetables, black beans, and a sprinkle of fresh cilantro. If using, add a pinch of chili powder and cumin for extra flavor.
4. Fold the tortilla in half over the filling. Press down gently with a spatula and cook for 2-3 minutes per side, or until golden brown and the cheese is melted. Repeat with the remaining tortillas and filling.
5. While the quesadillas cook, whisk together the plain, non-fat Greek yogurt, chopped fresh cilantro, lime juice, garlic powder, and black pepper in a small bowl.
6. Cut each quesadilla into wedges and serve them warm with the cilantro yogurt dip for dipping.

NOTES

- **Vegetable options:** Feel free to customize the vegetables based on your preferences. Other DASH-friendly options include chopped poblano pepper, corn kernels, or chopped spinach.
- **Cheese alternatives:** You can use a reduced-fat cheddar cheese or a blend of shredded mozzarella and low-fat cheddar cheese to add a different flavor profile.
- **Leftovers:** Leftover quesadillas can be stored in an airtight container in the refrigerator for up to 2 days. Reheat in a pan over medium heat or in the microwave until warmed through. The texture might be slightly less crispy.
- **Sodium content:** Be mindful of the sodium content in the cheese you use. Look for low-sodium options whenever possible.

NUTRITIONAL INFORMATION (approximate per serving):
Calories: 350 | Protein: 20g | Fat: 12g | Carbohydrates: 40g | Sodium: 450mg (depending on sodium content of ingredients) | Potassium: 500mg (depending on ingredients)

Vegetarian Stuffed Cabbage Rolls

These hearty vegetarian stuffed cabbage rolls are a delicious and nutritious option that fits perfectly into the DASH diet. Tender cabbage leaves are filled with a flavorful mixture of brown rice, lentils, vegetables, and herbs. This recipe keeps sodium in check by using low-sodium vegetable broth and focusing on natural flavors from the vegetables and spices.

 **Prep Time:** 30 minutes || **Cook Time:** 1 hour || **Yield:** 6-8 servings

INGREDIENTS

For the Cabbage Leaves:
- 1 head green cabbage (medium-sized)
- ¼ cup water

For the Filling:
- 1 cup cooked brown rice
- ½ cup cooked green lentils
- 1 cup chopped mushrooms (cremini, portobello, or your choice)
- ½ cup chopped onion
- ½ cup chopped carrots
- 1 clove garlic, minced
- 1 tablespoon olive oil
- ½ cup chopped fresh parsley
- ¼ cup chopped fresh dill (optional)
- 1 teaspoon dried thyme
- ½ teaspoon ground cumin
- Pinch of red pepper flakes (optional, for a spicy kick)
- Salt and freshly ground black pepper (optional) to taste
- ½ cup low-sodium vegetable broth

For the Simmering Sauce:
- 2 cups low-sodium vegetable broth
- 1 (14.5 oz) can diced tomatoes, undrained
- 1 tablespoon tomato paste

INSTRUCTIONS

1. Bring a large pot of water to a boil. Carefully remove the outer leaves of the cabbage. Using a sharp knife, core the cabbage, leaving the bottom intact.
2. Place the whole cabbage head in the boiling water. Cook for 5-7 minutes, or until the leaves begin to soften and wilt. Remove the cabbage with tongs and let it cool slightly. Separate the softened leaves from the head of cabbage. You will need about 12-16 large leaves.
3. In a large skillet, heat olive oil over medium heat. Add the chopped onion, carrots, and mushrooms. Cook for 5-7 minutes, or until softened. Add the minced garlic and cook for an additional minute.
4. Stir in the cooked brown rice, cooked green lentils, chopped fresh parsley, chopped fresh dill (if using), dried thyme, ground cumin, red pepper flakes (optional), salt, and freshly ground black pepper (optional) to taste.
5. Place about ⅓ cup of the filling mixture in the center of a blanched cabbage leaf. Fold the sides of the leaf inwards, then roll up tightly. Repeat with remaining cabbage leaves and filling mixture.
6. In a large pot or Dutch oven, combine the low-sodium vegetable broth, diced tomatoes (undrained), and tomato paste. Stir to combine.
7. Arrange the stuffed cabbage rolls snugly in a single layer in the pot with the simmering sauce. If needed, add a little extra water or vegetable broth to ensure the rolls are at least halfway submerged in the liquid. Bring the sauce to a simmer, then cover the pot and reduce heat to low. Simmer for 45-50 minutes, or until the cabbage leaves are tender and the filling is cooked through.
8. Carefully remove the cooked cabbage rolls from the pot with a slotted spoon and serve hot with your favorite sides, like roasted vegetables or a simple green salad. Enjoy the flavorful vegetarian twist on a classic comfort dish!

NOTES

- **Cabbage selection:** Choose a medium-sized head of green cabbage with firm leaves that are not too tough.
- **Cooking the lentils:** You can cook the green lentils from scratch or use pre-cooked lentils from the grocery store to save time.
- **Leftovers:** Leftover stuffed cabbage rolls can be stored in an airtight container in the refrigerator for up to 3 days. Reheat gently on the stovetop or in the microwave until warmed through.

NUTRITIONAL INFORMATION (approximate per serving):

Calories: 300 | Protein: 15g | Fat: 10g | Carbohydrates: 40g | Sodium: 400mg (depending on sodium content of ingredients) | Potassium: 700mg (depending on ingredients)

Hasselback Eggplant Parmesan

This recipe takes the classic eggplant parmesan and transforms it into a DASH-friendly delight! Packed with fiber-rich eggplant and protein-rich low-fat mozzarella, it features a flavorful tomato sauce and a crispy topping made with whole-wheat breadcrumbs. This recipe keeps sodium in check by using low-sodium alternatives and focusing on natural flavors.

 **Prep Time:** 15 minutes || **Cook Time:** 45-50 minutes || **Yield:** 2 servings

INGREDIENTS

For the Eggplant:
- 1 medium eggplant (about 1 pound)
- 1 tablespoon olive oil
- Freshly ground black pepper (optional)

For the Sauce:
- 1 tablespoon olive oil
- 1 clove garlic, minced
- 1 (14.5-oz) can diced tomatoes, undrained (fire-roasted tomatoes for added flavor)

- ½ teaspoon dried oregano
- Pinch of red pepper flakes (optional, for a spicy kick)

For the Topping:
- ½ cup whole-wheat breadcrumbs
- ¼ cup grated Parmesan cheese (optional)
- ¼ cup chopped fresh parsley
- Pinch of garlic powder

INSTRUCTIONS

1. Preheat your oven to 400°F (200°C). Lightly grease a baking sheet or line it with parchment paper for easier cleanup.
2. Wash the eggplant and pat it dry with paper towels. Place it upright on a cutting board. Using a sharp knife, carefully make lengthwise cuts along the eggplant, stopping just before you cut all the way through the bottom. The slices should be about ¼ inch thick.
3. Brush the eggplant with olive oil and season it lightly with freshly ground black pepper (optional) on both sides.
4. In a saucepan over medium heat, heat the olive oil. Add the minced garlic and cook for 30 seconds, or until fragrant. Stir in the diced tomatoes (undrained), dried oregano, and red pepper flakes (if using). Bring to a simmer and cook for 10 minutes, allowing the sauce to thicken slightly.
5. Spread a thin layer of the tomato sauce on the bottom of the prepared baking sheet. Place the prepared eggplant on the baking sheet, cut side up. Spoon the remaining tomato sauce evenly over the eggplant slices, filling the spaces in between.
6. In a small bowl, combine the whole-wheat breadcrumbs, grated Parmesan cheese (if using), chopped fresh parsley, and garlic powder. Mix well to combine.
7. Sprinkle the breadcrumb mixture evenly over the eggplant slices, making sure to get some in between the cuts.
8. Bake the eggplant parmesan in the preheated oven for 45-50 minutes, or until the eggplant is tender and cooked through, and the topping is golden brown and crispy.
9. Once cooked, carefully transfer the eggplant parmesan to serving plates. Let it cool slightly before serving. Enjoy it hot with a side salad or your favorite DASH-friendly vegetables.

NOTES
- **Eggplant selection:** Choose a medium-sized eggplant that feels firm and heavy for its size.
- **Parmesan cheese:** Grated Parmesan cheese adds a savory touch, but it's higher in sodium. Use a minimal amount or omit it entirely for a strictly low-sodium option. You can substitute with a low-sodium Parmesan cheese alternative if desired.

- **Leftovers:** Leftover eggplant parmesan can be stored in an airtight container in the refrigerator for up to 3 days. Reheat gently in the oven at 375°F (190°C) until warmed through. The topping might become slightly softer upon reheating.

NUTRITIONAL INFORMATION (approximate per serving, without Parmesan cheese):
Calories: 350 | Protein: 20g | Fat: 15g | Carbohydrates: 35g | Sodium: 400mg (depending on sodium content of ingredients) | Potassium: 500mg (depending on ingredients)

Curried Cauliflower Steaks with Red Rice & Tzatziki

This vibrant and flavorful dish is a perfect fit for the DASH diet. Tender cauliflower steaks are coated in a fragrant curry powder blend and roasted to perfection. The red rice provides a source of whole grains, while the refreshing tzatziki adds a cool and creamy counterpoint. This recipe keeps sodium in check by using low-sodium ingredients and focusing on natural herbs and spices.

 **Prep Time:** 15 minutes || **Cook Time:** 40-45 minutes || **Yield:** 4 servings

INGREDIENTS

For the Curried Cauliflower Steaks:
- 1 head cauliflower, medium-sized
- 1 tablespoon olive oil
- 1 teaspoon curry powder
- ½ teaspoon ground cumin
- ¼ teaspoon ground coriander
- Pinch of cayenne pepper (optional, for a spicy kick)
- ½ teaspoon garlic powder
- Salt and freshly ground black pepper (optional) to taste

For the Red Rice:

- 1 cup red rice, rinsed
- 1 ½ cups low-sodium vegetable broth

For the Tzatziki:
- ¾ cup plain, non-fat Greek yogurt
- ½ medium cucumber, seeded and grated
- 1 tablespoon chopped fresh dill
- 1 tablespoon chopped fresh mint (optional)
- 1 clove garlic, minced
- 1 tablespoon lemon juice
- Pinch of salt and freshly ground black pepper (optional) to taste

INSTRUCTIONS

1. Preheat your oven to 425°F (220°C). Line a baking sheet with parchment paper for easier cleanup.
2. Remove the outer leaves of the cauliflower, but keep the stem intact. Cut the cauliflower head vertically into steaks, about 1-inch thick.
3. In a small bowl, combine the olive oil, curry powder, ground cumin, ground coriander, cayenne pepper (if using), garlic powder, salt, and freshly ground black pepper (optional) to taste.
4. Brush the cauliflower steaks generously with the curry rub, coating them evenly on both sides.
5. Place the seasoned cauliflower steaks on the prepared baking sheet. Roast in the preheated oven for 30-35 minutes, or until the cauliflower is tender when pierced with a fork.
6. While the cauliflower roasts, cook the red rice according to package directions. Typically, you'll need to combine the rinsed red rice with the low-sodium vegetable broth in a pot, bring to a boil, then reduce heat, cover, and simmer for 40-45 minutes, or until the rice is cooked and fluffy.
7. In a medium bowl, whisk together the plain, non-fat Greek yogurt, grated cucumber, chopped fresh dill, chopped fresh mint (if using), minced garlic, lemon juice, salt, and freshly ground black pepper (optional) to taste. Stir until well combined and refrigerate for at least 15 minutes to allow the flavors to meld.
Tip: Taste the tzatziki before adding additional salt, as some brands of Greek yogurt might have higher sodium content.
8. Once the cauliflower steaks are roasted and the red rice is cooked, assemble your plates. Divide the cooked red rice among serving plates. Top with a curried cauliflower steak and a dollop of chilled tzatziki. Enjoy!

NOTES

- **Cauliflower selection:** Choose a medium-sized head of cauliflower with a firm and white head.
- **Red rice alternatives:** Brown rice can be used instead of red rice for a similar whole-grain option.
- **Leftovers:** Leftover curried cauliflower steaks, red rice, and tzatziki can be stored in separate airtight containers in the refrigerator for up to 3 days. Reheat gently in the oven or microwave until warmed through.

NUTRITIONAL INFORMATION (approximate per serving):
Calories: 400 | Protein: 15g | Fat: 10g | Carbohydrates: 55g | Sodium: 400mg (depending on sodium content of ingredients) | Potassium: 800mg (depending on ingredients)

Three Bean Chili with Vegetables and Spices

This flavorful three-bean chili is packed with protein and fiber from the beans, this recipe incorporates colorful vegetables and relies on low-sodium ingredients and spices for a delicious and nutritious dish.

 **Prep Time:** 10 minutes || **Cook Time:** 30-35 minutes || **Yield:** 4-6 servings

INGREDIENTS

For the Chili:
- 1 tablespoon olive oil
- 1 medium onion, chopped
- 1 green bell pepper, chopped
- 1 jalapeño pepper, seeded and diced (optional, for a spicy kick)
- 2 cloves garlic, minced
- 1 teaspoon ground cumin
- ½ teaspoon smoked paprika
- Pinch of dried oregano
- 1 (28-ounce) can crushed tomatoes, undrained
- 1 (15.5-ounce) can kidney beans, rinsed and drained
- 1 (15.5-ounce) can black beans, rinsed and drained
- 1 (15.5-ounce) can pinto beans, rinsed and drained
- 1 cup low-sodium vegetable broth
- ½ cup frozen corn
- 1 (4.5-ounce) can chopped green chiles (optional)
- Salt and freshly ground black pepper (optional) to taste

For Serving (optional):
- Chopped fresh cilantro
- Low-fat shredded cheddar cheese
- Low-fat Greek yogurt
- Avocado slices

INSTRUCTIONS

1. In a large pot or Dutch oven, heat olive oil over medium heat.
2. Add the chopped onion, green bell pepper, and jalapeño pepper (if using) to the hot oil. Sauté for 5-7 minutes, or until the vegetables are softened.
3. Stir in the ground cumin, smoked paprika, and dried oregano. Cook for an additional minute, allowing the spices to release their fragrance.
4. Pour in the crushed tomatoes (undrained), rinsed and drained kidney beans, black beans, and pinto beans. Add the low-sodium vegetable broth and stir to combine.
5. Bring the chili to a simmer, then reduce heat to low. Cover the pot and simmer for 20-25 minutes, or until the flavors meld and the chili thickens slightly.
6. Add the frozen corn and chopped green chiles (optional) to the pot. Stir to combine and simmer for an additional 5 minutes, or until the corn is heated through.
7. If desired, taste the chili and season with a pinch of salt and freshly ground black pepper (optional) to taste. You can add a little more water or vegetable broth if the chili seems too thick.
8. Ladle the hot chili into bowls. Serve with your favorite toppings like chopped fresh cilantro, low-fat shredded cheddar cheese, low-fat Greek yogurt, and avocado slices.

NOTES
- **Jalapeño pepper**: If you prefer a milder chili, omit the jalapeño pepper or remove the seeds before dicing.
- **Slow cooker option:** This chili can also be prepared in a slow cooker. Combine all ingredients in the slow cooker and cook on low for 6-8 hours, or on high for 4-5 hours.

NUTRITIONAL INFORMATION (approximate per serving):
Calories: 300 | Protein: 15g | Fat: 10g | Carbohydrates: 40g | Sodium: 450mg (depending on sodium content of ingredients) | Potassium: 800mg (depending on ingredients)

Chickpea and Potato Curry with Spinach

This flavorful chickpea and potato curry is a perfect example of a satisfying and nutritious meal that fits perfectly into the DASH diet. Packed with protein and fiber from the chickpeas, this recipe incorporates vegetables and relies on low-sodium ingredients and spices for a delicious and healthy dish.

 **Prep Time:** 10 minutes || **Cook Time:** 30-35 minutes || **Yield:** 4 servings

INGREDIENTS
For the Curry:
- 1 tablespoon olive oil
- 1 medium onion, chopped
- 1 green bell pepper, chopped
- 2 cloves garlic, minced
- 1 teaspoon ground cumin
- ½ teaspoon ground coriander
- Pinch of turmeric
- Pinch of red pepper flakes (optional)
- 1 (14.5-ounce) can diced tomatoes, undrained
- 1 (15.5-ounce) can chickpeas, drained and rinsed
- 2 medium potatoes, peeled and diced (about 2 cups)
- 1 cup low-sodium vegetable broth
- ½ cup chopped fresh spinach
- Salt and freshly ground black pepper (optional) to taste
- Chopped fresh cilantro (for garnish)

To Serve (optional):
- Cooked brown rice or quinoa
- Low-fat yogurt or raita (cucumber yogurt sauce)

INSTRUCTIONS
1. In a large pot or Dutch oven, heat olive oil over medium heat.
2. Add the chopped onion and green bell pepper to the hot oil. Sauté for 5-7 minutes, or until the vegetables are softened.
3. Stir in the ground cumin, ground coriander, turmeric, and red pepper flakes (optional). Cook for an additional minute, allowing the spices to release their fragrance.
4. Pour in the diced tomatoes (undrained), drained and rinsed chickpeas, and diced potatoes. Stir to combine.
5. Add the low-sodium vegetable broth and bring to a simmer. Cover the pot, reduce heat to low, and simmer for 15-20 minutes, or until the potatoes are tender.
6. Stir in the chopped fresh spinach and cook for an additional minute or two, or until the spinach is wilted.
7. If desired, taste the curry and season with a pinch of salt and freshly ground black pepper (optional) to taste. You can add a little more water or vegetable broth if the curry seems too thick.
8. Ladle the hot curry into bowls. Garnish with chopped fresh cilantro and serve with cooked brown rice or quinoa and a dollop of low-fat yogurt or raita (cucumber yogurt sauce) for an extra cooling touch.

NOTES
- **Vegetable options:** You can add other vegetables to the curry, such as chopped carrots, zucchini, or peas.
- **Spinach variation:** Frozen chopped spinach, thawed and squeezed to remove excess moisture, can be used instead of fresh spinach.
- **Spice level:** Adjust the amount of red pepper flakes to your preference for spiciness.

- **Leftovers:** Leftover chickpea and potato curry can be stored in an airtight container in the refrigerator for up to 3 days. Reheat gently on the stovetop or in the microwave until warmed through.

NUTRITIONAL INFORMATION (approximate per serving):
Calories: 350 | Protein: 15g | Fat: 10g | Carbohydrates: 45g | Sodium: 400mg (depending on sodium content of ingredients) | Potassium: 700mg (depending on ingredients)

Lentil and Bean Casserole with Vegetables

This flavorful casserole offers a protein-packed and fiber-rich alternative to traditional baked beans with ground beef. Lentils and cannellini beans provide a satisfying base, while vegetables and herbs add flavor and nutrients. This recipe keeps sodium in check by using low-sodium ingredients and focusing on natural flavors.

 **Prep Time:** 15 minutes || **Cook Time:** 45-50 minutes || **Yield:** 4-6 servings

INGREDIENTS
For the Casserole:
- 1 tablespoon olive oil
- 1 medium onion, chopped
- 1 green bell pepper, chopped
- 1 carrot, chopped
- 2 cloves garlic, minced
- 1 teaspoon ground cumin
- ½ teaspoon dried thyme
- Pinch of red pepper flakes (optional)
- 1 (15.5-ounce) can diced tomatoes, undrained
- 1 cup cooked brown lentils
- 1 (15.5-ounce) can cannellini beans, rinsed and drained
- 1 cup low-sodium vegetable broth
- ½ cup frozen corn
- ½ cup chopped fresh parsley
- Salt and freshly ground black pepper (optional) to taste

For the Topping (optional):
- ½ cup whole wheat bread crumbs
- 1 tablespoon olive oil

INSTRUCTIONS
1. Preheat your oven to 375°F (190°C).
2. In a large skillet or Dutch oven, heat olive oil over medium heat.
3. Sauté the vegetables: Add the chopped onion, green bell pepper, and carrot to the hot oil. Sauté for 5-7 minutes, or until the vegetables are softened.
4. Add spices and garlic: Stir in the ground cumin, dried thyme, and red pepper flakes (optional). Cook for an additional minute, allowing the spices to release their fragrance.
5. Pour in the diced tomatoes (undrained), cooked brown lentils, and rinsed and drained cannellini beans. Stir to combine.
6. Bring the mixture to a simmer, then reduce heat to low. Cover the pot and simmer for 10 minutes. Add the low-sodium vegetable broth and stir to combine.
7. Increase heat to medium and bring to a simmer again. Simmer for an additional 15-20 minutes, or until the lentils and beans are heated through and the sauce has thickened slightly. Stir in the frozen corn and cook for an additional 2-3 minutes, or until the corn is heated through.
8. If desired, taste the casserole and season with a pinch of salt and freshly ground black pepper (optional) to taste. In a small bowl, combine the whole wheat bread crumbs with 1 tablespoon olive oil.
9. Transfer the lentil and bean mixture to a baking dish. If using the topping, sprinkle the bread crumb mixture evenly over the top of the casserole. Bake for 15-20 minutes, or until the topping is golden brown and crisp.
10. Serve the hot casserole with a sprinkle of chopped fresh parsley.

NOTES
- **Ground beef substitution**: If you still prefer some meat, consider using a very small amount of lean ground turkey or chicken sausage, browned and crumbled, but be mindful of the added sodium content.

- **Leftovers:** Leftover lentil and bean casserole can be stored in an airtight container in the refrigerator for up to 3 days. Reheat gently on the stovetop or in the microwave until warmed through.

NUTRITIONAL INFORMATION (approximate per serving, without topping):
Calories: 350 | Protein: 18g | Fat: 10g | Carbohydrates: 45g | Sodium: 400mg (depending on sodium content of ingredients) | Potassium: 800mg (depending on ingredients

Pork Chops with Light Tomato Curry

This flavorful curry recipe is perfect for the DASH diet by focusing on lean protein, low-sodium ingredients, and a vibrant tomato base. Tender pork chops are simmered in a fragrant curry with vegetables, creating a satisfying and nutritious meal.

 **Prep Time:** 15 minutes ||  **Cook Time:** 30-35 minutes ||  **Yield:** 4 servings

INGREDIENTS

For the Pork Chops:
- 4 bone-in pork chops (loin or rib chops, trimmed)
- 1 tablespoon olive oil
- ½ teaspoon ground cumin
- Pinch of paprika
- Pinch of salt and freshly ground black pepper (optional)

For the Tomato Curry:
- 1 tablespoon olive oil
- 1 medium onion, chopped
- 1 clove garlic, minced
- 1 teaspoon grated ginger
- 1 (14.5 oz) can diced tomatoes, undrained (fire-roasted recommended for added flavor)
- 1 cup low-sodium vegetable broth
- ½ teaspoon curry powder
- ¼ teaspoon ground turmeric
- Pinch of cayenne pepper (optional)
- 1 bay leaf
- ½ cup chopped fresh cilantro

INSTRUCTIONS

1. In a bowl, toss the pork chops with olive oil, ground cumin, paprika, and a pinch of salt and freshly ground black pepper (optional).
2. Heat a large skillet over medium-high heat. Add the olive oil and sear the pork chops for 2-3 minutes per side, or until browned.
3. Reduce heat to medium. Add the chopped onion and cook for 3-4 minutes, or until softened. Stir in the minced garlic and grated ginger, and cook for an additional minute.
4. Add the diced tomatoes (undrained), low-sodium vegetable broth, curry powder, ground turmeric, cayenne pepper (optional), and bay leaf to the skillet. Bring to a simmer, scraping up any browned bits from the bottom of the pan.
5. Carefully nestle the seasoned pork chops back into the skillet, ensuring they are mostly submerged in the liquid. Cover and simmer for 20-25 minutes, or until the pork chops are cooked through and tender.
6. Once cooked, remove the bay leaf and stir in the chopped fresh cilantro.
7. Serve the pork chops with the flavorful tomato curry sauce spooned over them. You can enjoy this dish with a side of brown rice, quinoa, or roasted vegetables for a complete meal.

NOTES
- **Trimming pork chops:** Trim any excess fat from the pork chops before cooking.
- **Bone-in vs. boneless:** Bone-in pork chops add extra flavor to the dish, but you can use boneless pork chops if preferred. Adjust cooking time slightly depending on thickness.
- **Sodium content:** Choose low-sodium vegetable broth and diced tomatoes to keep sodium in check. You can adjust the amount of cayenne pepper (optional) to your spice preference.

NUTRITIONAL INFORMATION (approximate per serving):
Calories: 400 | Protein: 30g | Fat: 15g | Carbohydrates: 30g | Sodium: 500mg (depending on sodium content of ingredients) | Potassium: 700mg (depending on ingredients)

Chickpea Pasta with Mushrooms, Kale, and Cherry Tomatoes

This flavorful and satisfying dish combines protein-rich chickpea pasta, hearty mushrooms, and nutrient-packed kale with a light and flavorful lemon-garlic sauce. Perfect for the DASH diet, it delivers a delicious and nutritious meal that keeps sodium in check.

 **Prep Time:** 15 minutes || **Cook Time:** 20-25 minutes || **Yield:** 4 servings

INGREDIENTS

For the Pasta:
- 8 ounces chickpea rotini or penne pasta (see Tip below)
- 4 cups water

For the Vegetables and Sauce:
- 1 tablespoon olive oil
- 8 ounces cremini mushrooms, sliced
- 2 cloves garlic, minced
- 8 cups chopped kale
- ½ teaspoon dried thyme
- Pinch of red pepper flakes (optional)
- ¼ cup low-sodium vegetable broth
- ¼ cup freshly squeezed lemon juice
- 1 tablespoon grated Parmesan cheese (optional, for garnish)
- Salt and freshly ground black pepper to taste (optional)
- ½ cup cherry tomatoes, halved (optional)

INSTRUCTIONS

1. In a large pot, bring 4 cups of water to a boil. Add the chickpea pasta and cook, usually for 8-10 minutes, or until al dente (cooked but still firm to the bite). Reserve 1 cup of the pasta cooking water before draining.
2. While the pasta cooks, heat olive oil in a large skillet or pan over medium heat. Add the sliced cremini mushrooms and cook for 5-7 minutes, or until softened and golden brown.
3. Stir in the minced garlic and dried thyme to the pan with the cooked mushrooms. Cook for an additional minute to release the fragrance of the garlic. Add a pinch of red pepper flakes (optional) for a touch of heat.
4. Add the chopped kale to the pan with the mushrooms and spices. Pour in the low-sodium vegetable broth and stir to combine. Cover the pan and cook for 2-3 minutes, or until the kale is wilted and tender.
5. Once the kale is wilted, add the reserved pasta cooking water and freshly squeezed lemon juice to the pan. Stir in the drained chickpea pasta and toss to coat with the sauce.
6. Taste the dish and adjust seasonings with salt and freshly ground black pepper as desired. Remember, the vegetable broth might contribute some sodium, so taste before adding additional salt.
7. Divide the chickpea pasta with mushrooms, kale, and lemon-garlic sauce among serving plates. Top with halved cherry tomatoes (optional) and a sprinkle of grated Parmesan cheese (optional) for a finishing touch. Serve hot and enjoy!

NOTES
- **Chickpea pasta selection:** Choose a chickpea pasta made from 100% chickpea flour for the most protein and fiber.
- **Vegetable options:** Feel free to customize the vegetables based on your preferences. Other DASH-friendly options include chopped zucchini, chopped broccoli florets, or a handful of spinach added towards the end of cooking with the kale.
- **Cherry tomatoes:** Adding cherry tomatoes brings a pop of color and freshness, but they are optional.

- **Parmesan cheese:** Grated Parmesan cheese adds a savory touch, but it's higher in sodium. Use a minimal amount or omit it entirely for a strictly low-sodium option.

NUTRITIONAL INFORMATION (approximate per serving, without Parmesan cheese and cherry tomatoes):
Calories: 350 | Protein: 18g | Fat: 10g | Carbohydrates: 40g | Sodium: 300mg (depending on sodium content of ingredients) | Potassium: 500mg (depending on ingredients)

Black Bean and Sweet Potato Rice Bowls with Cilantro Lime Vinaigrette

These vibrant bowls offer a packed with protein and fiber from black beans and sweet potatoes, this recipe keeps sodium content in check and uses flavorful spices for a healthy and satisfying dish.

 **Prep Time:** 15 minutes || **Cook Time:** 30-35 minutes || **Yield:** 2 servings

INGREDIENTS

For the Sweet Potatoes:
- 1 medium sweet potato, peeled and diced (about 2 cups)
- 1 tablespoon olive oil
- ½ teaspoon ground cumin
- Pinch of chili powder (optional)
- Pinch of salt and freshly ground black pepper (optional)

For the Cilantro Lime Vinaigrette:
- 2 tablespoons olive oil
- 2 tablespoons fresh lime juice
- 1 tablespoon chopped fresh cilantro
- 1 teaspoon Dijon mustard
- Pinch of garlic powder
- Pinch of salt and freshly ground black pepper (optional)

For the Bowls:
- 1 cup cooked brown rice (or quinoa)
- 1 can (15 oz) black beans, rinsed and drained
- ½ cup chopped avocado (optional)
- ¼ cup chopped fresh cilantro
- Chopped red onion (optional)
- Lime wedges (for serving)

INSTRUCTIONS
1. Preheat your oven to 400°F (200°C).
2. In a bowl, toss the diced sweet potatoes with olive oil, ground cumin, chili powder (optional), and a pinch of salt and freshly ground black pepper (optional).
3. Spread the seasoned sweet potatoes on a baking sheet and roast in the preheated oven for 20-25 minutes, or until tender-crisp.
4. In a small bowl, whisk together olive oil, lime juice, chopped fresh cilantro, Dijon mustard, garlic powder, and a pinch of salt and freshly ground black pepper (optional).
5. Divide the cooked brown rice (or quinoa) between two bowls. Top each bowl with roasted sweet potatoes, black beans, chopped avocado (optional), chopped fresh cilantro, and chopped red onion (optional).
6. Drizzle each bowl with desired amount of cilantro lime vinaigrette.
7. Serve the bowls with lime wedges for squeezing additional fresh lime juice over the ingredients, if desired.

NOTES
- **Roasting variations:** You can also roast the sweet potatoes in cubes or wedges instead of dicing them.
- **Avocado variations:** To prevent browning, you can toss the avocado cubes with a little lime juice before adding them to the bowls.

NUTRITIONAL INFORMATION (approximate per serving, without avocado):
Calories: 450 | Protein: 15g | Fat: 15g | Carbohydrates: 60g | Sodium: 400mg (depending on sodium content of ingredients) | Potassium: 800mg (depending on ingredients)

Portobello Florentine with Light Cream Sauce and Spinach

This vegetarian recipe is a perfect addition to the DASH diet. Hearty portobello mushroom caps are filled with a creamy spinach mixture made with low-fat ricotta cheese and flavored with fresh herbs. Baked to tender perfection, this dish offers a satisfying and flavorful main course that keeps sodium content in check.

 **Prep Time:** 15 minutes || **Cook Time:** 20-25 minutes || **Yield:** 2 servings

INGREDIENTS

For the Portobello Mushrooms:
- 2 large portobello mushroom caps (about 4-5 inches in diameter)
- 1 tablespoon olive oil
- Pinch of dried thyme
- Pinch of garlic powder
- Salt and freshly ground black pepper (optional, to taste)

For the Spinach Filling:
- 1 tablespoon olive oil
- 1 shallot, minced
- 2 cloves garlic, minced
- 5 ounces fresh spinach, chopped
- ½ cup low-fat ricotta cheese
- 2 tablespoons grated Parmesan cheese (optional)
- ¼ cup low-sodium vegetable broth
- 1 tablespoon chopped fresh parsley
- Pinch of dried nutmeg (optional)
- Pinch of salt and freshly ground black pepper (optional, to taste)

INSTRUCTIONS

1. Preheat your oven to 400°F (200°C). Carefully remove the stems from the portobello mushroom caps. Brush the caps with olive oil and sprinkle them with dried thyme, garlic powder, and a pinch of salt and freshly ground black pepper (optional, to taste). Place the portobello caps, gill-side down, on a baking sheet.
2. In a skillet, heat olive oil over medium heat. Add the minced shallot and cook for 2-3 minutes, or until softened. Stir in the minced garlic and cook for an additional minute.
3. Add the chopped fresh spinach to the skillet and cook until wilted. Season with a pinch of salt and freshly ground black pepper (optional, to taste).
4. In a bowl, combine the wilted spinach, low-fat ricotta cheese, grated Parmesan cheese (optional), low-sodium vegetable broth, chopped fresh parsley, and a pinch of dried nutmeg (optional). Stir well to combine.
5. Divide the spinach filling mixture evenly between the portobello mushroom caps.
6. Bake the stuffed portobello mushrooms in the preheated oven for 15-20 minutes, or until the filling is heated through and the tops start to brown slightly. If desired, you can broil the tops of the mushrooms for an additional minute or two for a crispier topping.
7. Carefully transfer the portobello Florentine to serving plates. Serve immediately and enjoy!

NOTES
- **Portobello size:** Choose portobello mushroom caps that are large enough to hold the filling comfortably.
- **Ricotta cheese alternatives:** If you cannot find low-fat ricotta cheese, you can substitute it with cottage cheese or mashed low-fat feta cheese.

NUTRITIONAL INFORMATION (approximate per serving, without Parmesan cheese):
Calories: 300 | Protein: 20g | Fat: 15g | Carbohydrates: 15g | Sodium: 400mg (depending on sodium content of ingredients) | Potassium: 800mg (depending on ingredients)

Peppered Sole with Lemon and Herbs

This light and flavorful dish is perfect for the DASH diet. Pan-seared sole fillets are seasoned with a cracked pepper mixture and complemented by a touch of lemon and fresh herbs. Simple yet satisfying, this recipe keeps sodium content in check while offering a delicious and healthy main course.

Prep Time: 10 minutes || **Cook Time:** 10-12 minutes || **Yield:** 2 servings

INGREDIENTS
For the Sole:
- 2 sole fillets (6-8 ounces each)
- 1 tablespoon olive oil
- ½ teaspoon black peppercorns, crushed (or ½ teaspoon ground black pepper)
- Pinch of dried thyme
- Pinch of freshly ground nutmeg (optional)

- Salt (optional, to taste)

For the Garnish (optional):
- 1 tablespoon fresh lemon juice
- 1 tablespoon chopped fresh parsley
- Lemon wedges (for serving)

INSTRUCTIONS
1. Pat the sole fillets dry with paper towels. Season them lightly with salt (optional), if using.
2. Using a mortar and pestle or a spice grinder, crush the black peppercorns until coarsely ground. Alternatively, you can substitute ½ teaspoon of pre-ground black pepper.
3. In a shallow dish, combine the crushed black peppercorns (or ground black pepper), dried thyme, and a pinch of freshly ground nutmeg (optional). Dredge the sole fillets in the pepper mixture, coating them evenly.
4. In a large nonstick skillet, heat olive oil over medium heat.
5. Carefully place the seasoned sole fillets in the hot skillet. Cook for 3-4 minutes per side, or until golden brown and the fish flakes easily with a fork. Avoid overcooking the fish.
6. Once the fish is cooked, you can optionally deglaze the pan for a flavorful sauce. Add a tablespoon of white wine or low-sodium chicken broth to the pan and scrape up any browned bits. Let it simmer for a minute and reduce slightly.
7. Transfer the cooked sole fillets to serving plates. Spoon any pan sauce (optional) over the fish. Drizzle with fresh lemon juice (optional) and garnish with chopped fresh parsley. Serve with lemon wedges for squeezing additional fresh lemon juice over the fish, if desired.

NOTES
- **Sole selection:** Choose firm and light-colored sole fillets for the best results.
- **Alternative herbs:** You can substitute other fresh herbs like dill, chives, or oregano for the dried thyme.
- **Leftovers:** Leftover cooked sole can be stored in an airtight container in the refrigerator for up to 2 days. Reheat gently on the stovetop over low heat until warmed through.

NUTRITIONAL INFORMATION (approximate per serving, without optional garnishes):
Calories: 250 | Protein: 30g | Fat: 10g | Carbohydrates: 0g | Sodium: 50mg (depending on sodium content of ingredients) | Potassium: 500mg (depending on ingredients)

White Beans and Bow Ties with Herbs

This flavorful and protein-packed dish is a perfect addition to your DASH diet meal plan. Combining cannellini beans for protein and fiber with whole-wheat bow ties and a light and flavorful tomato sauce seasoned with fresh herbs, it delivers a satisfying meal that keeps sodium in check.

 **Prep Time:** 15 minutes ||  **Cook Time:** 20-25 minutes ||  **Yield:** 4 servings

INGREDIENTS

- 1 tablespoon olive oil
- 1 medium onion, chopped
- 2 cloves garlic, minced
- 1 (14.5 oz) can diced tomatoes, undrained (fire-roasted or petite diced recommended)
- 1 (15 oz) can cannellini beans, drained and rinsed
- 4 cups low-sodium chicken broth
- 8 ounces whole-wheat bow tie pasta

- ¼ cup chopped fresh parsley
- 2 tablespoons chopped fresh basil
- ½ teaspoon dried oregano
- Pinch of red pepper flakes (optional)
- Freshly ground black pepper to taste
- Chopped fresh parsley (additional, for garnish)
- Shredded Parmesan cheese (optional, for garnish)

INSTRUCTIONS

1. Heat the olive oil in a large pot or Dutch oven over medium heat. Add the chopped onion and cook for 5 minutes, or until softened. Stir in the minced garlic and cook for an additional 30 seconds, until fragrant.
2. Add the diced tomatoes with their juices and the low-sodium chicken broth to the pot. Bring to a simmer.
3. Add the whole-wheat bow tie pasta and rinsed cannellini beans to the simmering broth mixture.
4. Cook for 15-20 minutes, or until the pasta is al dente (slightly firm to the bite) and the beans are heated through.
5. Stir in the chopped fresh parsley, chopped fresh basil, and dried oregano.
6. Season with a pinch of red pepper flakes (optional) and freshly ground black pepper to taste. Avoid adding salt initially, considering the sodium content of the broth and canned goods. Taste and adjust if needed.
7. Ladle the white beans and bow ties with herbs into bowls. Garnish with additional chopped fresh parsley (optional) and a sprinkle of shredded Parmesan cheese (optional).

NOTES

- **Fresh or dried herbs:** Fresh herbs offer the most vibrant flavor, but dried herbs can be substituted in a pinch. Use 1 teaspoon dried parsley, 1 teaspoon dried basil, and a pinch of dried oregano for the equivalent of the fresh herbs.
- **Leftovers:** Leftover white beans and bow ties can be stored in an airtight container in the refrigerator for up to 3 days. Reheat gently on the stovetop over low heat until warmed through.

NUTRITIONAL INFORMATION (approximate per serving, without Parmesan cheese):
Calories: 400 | Protein: 18g | Fat: 12g | Carbohydrates: 55g | Sodium: 450mg (depending on sodium content of ingredients) | Potassium: 700mg (depending on ingredients)

Italian Turkey Sausage Stuffed Zucchini with Light Tomato Sauce

This recipe takes inspiration from the classic Italian sausage stuffed zucchini, but with adjustments to make it more DASH-friendly. Here, we focus on using lean ground turkey sausage and a light tomato sauce made with fresh ingredients, keeping sodium content in check while offering a flavorful and satisfying meal.

Prep Time: 15 minutes || **Cook Time:** 30-35 minutes || **Yield:** 4 servings

INGREDIENTS

For the Zucchini:
- 4 medium zucchini (about 8 ounces each)
- 1 tablespoon olive oil

For the Sausage Stuffing:
- 1 pound ground turkey sausage (at least 90% lean)
- ½ cup chopped onion
- ½ cup chopped bell pepper (red, yellow, or orange)
- 2 cloves garlic, minced
- ½ cup chopped mushrooms (optional)
- ½ cup cooked brown rice (or quinoa)
- ¼ cup chopped fresh parsley
- 1 tablespoon grated Parmesan cheese (optional)
- Pinch of dried oregano
- Pinch of salt and freshly ground black pepper (optional)

For the Light Tomato Sauce:
- 1 tablespoon olive oil
- 1 (14.5 oz) can diced tomatoes, undrained (fire-roasted recommended for added flavor)
- ½ cup low-sodium vegetable broth
- ½ teaspoon dried basil
- Pinch of garlic powder
- Pinch of salt and freshly ground black pepper (optional)

INSTRUCTIONS

1. Preheat your oven to 400°F (200°C).
2. Wash and dry the zucchini. Cut them in half lengthwise and scoop out the flesh, leaving a 1/4-inch border around the edges. Reserve the zucchini flesh for the stuffing (optional) or discard.
3. Brush the hollowed zucchini halves with olive oil and place them cut-side down on a baking sheet. Bake for 5-7 minutes, or until slightly softened.
4. While the zucchini bakes, heat a large skillet over medium heat. Add the ground turkey sausage and cook until browned, breaking it up with a spoon as it cooks. Drain any excess grease.
5. Add the chopped onion, bell pepper, and minced garlic to the skillet with the cooked sausage. Sauté for 3-4 minutes, or until softened. Stir in the chopped mushrooms (optional).
6. Add the cooked brown rice (or quinoa), chopped fresh parsley, grated Parmesan cheese (optional), dried oregano, and a pinch of salt and freshly ground black pepper (optional) to the skillet. Mix well to combine.
7. In a separate saucepan, heat olive oil over medium heat. Add the diced tomatoes (undrained), low-sodium vegetable broth, dried basil, garlic powder, and a pinch of salt and freshly ground black pepper (optional). Bring to a simmer and cook for 5-7 minutes, or until slightly thickened.
8. Spoon the sausage stuffing mixture into the pre-baked zucchini halves. Pour a light amount of the tomato sauce over each stuffed zucchini.
9. Bake the stuffed zucchini for 15-20 minutes, or until heated through and the sauce is bubbly.
10. Serve the stuffed zucchini with additional tomato sauce on the side, if desired.

NOTES

- **Reserve zucchini flesh:** You can chop the reserved zucchini flesh and add it to the sausage stuffing mixture for extra veggies.
- **Brown rice vs. quinoa:** Both brown rice and quinoa offer whole grains and fiber. Choose whichever you prefer.
- **Feta cheese alternative:** For a sprinkle of salty flavor without excessive sodium, you can crumble a small amount of low-fat feta cheese over the finished dish before serving (optional).
- **Leftovers:** Leftover stuffed zucchini and tomato sauce can be stored in separate airtight containers in the refrigerator for up to 3 days. Reheat gently on the stovetop until warmed through.

NUTRITIONAL INFORMATION (approximate per serving, without Parmesan cheese and feta cheese):
Calories: 400 | Protein: 30g | Fat: 15g | Carbohydrates: 35g | Sodium: 500mg (depending on sodium content of ingredients) | Potassium: 800mg (depending on ingredients)

Shrimp Orzo with Lemon-Herb Feta

This vibrant dish offers a delightful combination of tender shrimp, toothsome orzo pasta, and creamy feta cheese crumbles, all adhering to the DASH diet. Packed with protein and fiber, this recipe keeps sodium content in check by using low-sodium ingredients and fresh flavors.

 **Prep Time:** 15 minutes || **Cook Time:** 20-25 minutes || **Yield:** 2 servings

INGREDIENTS

For the Orzo:
- 1 cup orzo pasta
- 4 cups low-sodium vegetable broth
- 1 tablespoon olive oil
- Pinch of dried oregano
- Pinch of garlic powder
- Salt and freshly ground black pepper (optional, to taste)

For the Shrimp and Feta:
- 4 ounces raw shrimp, peeled and deveined (deveining optional)
- 1 tablespoon olive oil
- ½ teaspoon dried thyme
- Pinch of paprika
- ¼ cup crumbled low-fat feta cheese
- 2 tablespoons chopped fresh parsley

INSTRUCTIONS

1. In a medium saucepan, heat olive oil over medium heat. Add the orzo and cook for 1 minute, stirring constantly to toast the pasta slightly. Pour in the low-sodium vegetable broth, dried oregano, garlic powder, and a pinch of salt and freshly ground black pepper (optional, to taste). Bring to a boil, then reduce heat and simmer for 15-20 minutes, or until the orzo is cooked through and the broth is absorbed.
2. While the orzo cooks, heat another tablespoon of olive oil in a large skillet over medium heat. Season the shrimp with dried thyme and paprika. Add the shrimp to the skillet and cook for 3-4 minutes per side, or until pink and cooked through.
3. Once the orzo is cooked, remove it from the heat. Stir in the cooked shrimp, crumbled low-fat feta cheese, and chopped fresh parsley. Gently toss to combine.
4. Transfer the shrimp orzo with feta to serving plates. Enjoy immediately while the flavors are fresh.

NOTES
- **Shrimp size:** Adjust the cooking time slightly depending on the size of the shrimp you use.
- **Feta alternatives:** If feta cheese is not available, you can substitute it with crumbled low-fat ricotta cheese or a sprinkle of grated Parmesan cheese.
- **Fresh herbs:** Fresh herbs like dill or chives can be used instead of parsley for a different flavor profile.
- **Leftovers:** Leftover shrimp orzo with feta can be stored in an airtight container in the refrigerator for up to 2 days. Reheat gently on the stovetop until warmed through.

NUTRITIONAL INFORMATION (approximate per serving, without optional salt and pepper): Calories: 400 | Protein: 30g | Fat: 15g | Carbohydrates: 40g | Sodium: 500mg (depending on sodium content of ingredients) | Potassium: 700mg (depending on ingredients)

Grilled Tilapia with Light and Tangy Pineapple Salsa

This recipe is a perfect example of a flavorful and satisfying meal that perfectly fits the DASH diet. Grilled tilapia fillets are paired with a vibrant pineapple salsa made with fresh ingredients, keeping sodium content in check while offering a delicious and refreshing combination.

Prep Time: 15 minutes || **Cook Time:** 10-12 minutes || **Yield:** 2 servings

INGREDIENTS
For the Tilapia:
- 2 tilapia fillets (4-6 ounces each)
- 1 tablespoon olive oil
- ½ teaspoon dried thyme
- Pinch of paprika
- Pinch of garlic powder
- Salt and freshly ground black pepper (optional, to taste)

For the Pineapple Salsa:
- 1 cup fresh pineapple, diced
- ½ cup chopped red bell pepper
- ¼ cup chopped red onion
- 1 tablespoon chopped fresh cilantro
- 1 tablespoon fresh lime juice
- 1 teaspoon olive oil
- Pinch of chili powder (optional)

INSTRUCTIONS
1. In a shallow dish, combine olive oil, dried thyme, paprika, garlic powder, and a pinch of salt and freshly ground black pepper (optional). Add the tilapia fillets and coat them evenly with the marinade. Let them sit for 10 minutes (optional) to infuse flavor.
2. In a bowl, combine the diced fresh pineapple, chopped red bell pepper, chopped red onion, chopped fresh cilantro, fresh lime juice, olive oil, and a pinch of chili powder (optional). Stir well to combine.
3. Preheat your grill to medium-high heat (around 400°F).
4. Lightly oil the grill grates. Carefully place the tilapia fillets on the preheated grill. Grill for 3-4 minutes per side, or until cooked through and the fish flakes easily with a fork. Avoid overcooking the fish.
5. Transfer the grilled tilapia to serving plates. Spoon the fresh pineapple salsa over the fish. Serve with a side of brown rice, quinoa, or roasted vegetables for a complete meal.

NOTES
- **Tilapia selection:** Choose firm and light-colored tilapia fillets for the best results.
- **Grill pan alternative:** If you don't have a grill, you can cook the tilapia in a grill pan over medium heat on your stovetop.
- **Salsa variations:** You can add a jalapeno pepper (seeded and minced) to the salsa for a touch of heat.
- **Leftovers:** Leftover cooked tilapia can be stored in an airtight container in the refrigerator for up to 2 days. Reheat gently on the stovetop or in the microwave until warmed through. The salsa is best enjoyed fresh.

NUTRITIONAL INFORMATION (approximate per serving, without optional salt and pepper): Calories: 350 | Protein: 30g | Fat: 10g | Carbohydrates: 30g | Sodium: 400mg (depending on sodium content of ingredients) | Potassium: 700mg (depending on ingredients)

California Quinoa with Light Vinaigrette and Fresh Herbs

This California quinoa recipe is packed with protein and fiber-rich quinoa, this dish features a variety of colorful vegetables and a light vinaigrette dressing, keeping sodium content in check while offering a vibrant and refreshing accompaniment to your meals.

 **Prep Time:** 15 minutes || **Cook Time:** 15-20 minutes || **Yield:** 4 servings

INGREDIENTS

For the Quinoa:
- 1 cup quinoa, rinsed
- 1 ½ cups low-sodium vegetable broth
- Pinch of dried thyme
- Pinch of garlic powder

For the California Mix:
- 1 cup chopped tomatoes (such as Roma or cherry)
- ½ cup chopped cucumber
- ½ cup chopped avocado
- ¼ cup chopped red onion
- ¼ cup chopped fresh parsley
- 2 tablespoons crumbled low-fat feta cheese (optional)

For the Light Vinaigrette:
- 2 tablespoons olive oil
- 1 tablespoon fresh lemon juice
- 1 teaspoon white wine vinegar (optional)
- Pinch of dried oregano
- Pinch of salt and freshly ground black pepper (optional)

INSTRUCTIONS

1. In a medium saucepan, combine the rinsed quinoa, low-sodium vegetable broth, dried thyme, and garlic powder. Bring to a boil, then reduce heat and simmer for 15-20 minutes, or until the quinoa is cooked through and the liquid is absorbed. Fluff the quinoa with a fork and set aside to cool slightly.
2. While the quinoa cooks, chop the tomatoes, cucumber, avocado, red onion, and fresh parsley. In a large bowl, combine the chopped vegetables and herbs.
3. In a small bowl, whisk together the olive oil, fresh lemon juice, white wine vinegar (optional), dried oregano, and a pinch of salt and freshly ground black pepper (optional).
4. Once the quinoa is cool, add it to the bowl with the chopped vegetables and herbs. Pour the light vinaigrette over the mixture and toss gently to combine.
5. Transfer the California quinoa salad to a serving dish. Top with crumbled low-fat feta cheese (optional) for a touch of salty flavor. Serve immediately and enjoy!

NOTES
- **Quinoa rinsing:** Rinsing quinoa removes any bitter coating from the outer layer of the grains.
- **Vegetable variations:** You can add other chopped vegetables to the California mix, such as chopped bell peppers, zucchini, or corn.
- **Vinaigrette variations:** You can use balsamic vinegar instead of white wine vinegar for a slightly different flavor profile.
- **Feta cheese alternative:** If feta cheese is not available, you can omit it or substitute it with a sprinkle of grated Parmesan cheese.

NUTRITIONAL INFORMATION (approximate per serving, without feta cheese and optional salt and pepper):
Calories: 300 | Protein: 8g | Fat: 10g | Carbohydrates: 40g | Sodium: 300mg (depending on sodium content of ingredients) | Potassium: 500mg (depending on ingredients)

Peppered Tuna Kabobs with Lemon and Herbs

These flavorful tuna kabobs are a perfect addition to the DASH diet. Marinated in a light and flavorful blend of herbs and spices, the tuna cooks up tender and juicy. Paired with colorful vegetables and grilled to perfection, this dish offers a satisfying and healthy main course that keeps sodium content in check.

 **Prep Time:** 15 minutes ||  **Cook Time:** 10-12 minutes ||  **Yield:** 4 servings

INGREDIENTS

For the Marinade:
- 2 tablespoons olive oil
- 1 tablespoon fresh lemon juice
- ½ teaspoon dried thyme
- ½ teaspoon dried oregano
- Pinch of garlic powder
- Pinch of freshly ground black pepper
- ¼ teaspoon crushed red pepper flakes (optional)

For the Kabobs:
- 1 pound fresh tuna steaks, cut into 1-inch cubes

- 1 bell pepper (red, yellow, or orange), cut into 1-inch squares
- 1 red onion, cut into 1-inch wedges
- 1 zucchini, cut into 1-inch cubes (optional)
- 1 summer squash, cut into 1-inch cubes (optional)
- Cherry tomatoes (optional)
- Wooden skewers (soaked in water for 10 minutes to prevent burning)

For Serving (optional):
- Lemon wedges
- Chopped fresh parsley

INSTRUCTIONS

1. In a shallow dish, whisk together the olive oil, fresh lemon juice, dried thyme, dried oregano, garlic powder, freshly ground black pepper, and crushed red pepper flakes (optional).
2. Add the tuna cubes to the marinade and toss to coat them evenly. Let them marinate for at least 15 minutes, or up to 30 minutes for deeper flavor.
3. While the tuna marinates, prepare the vegetables by cutting the bell pepper, red onion, zucchini (optional), summer squash (optional), and cherry tomatoes (optional) into similar bite-sized pieces.
4. Thread the marinated tuna cubes and vegetables alternately onto the soaked wooden skewers.
5. Preheat your grill to medium-high heat (around 400°F).
6. Grill the kabobs for 3-4 minutes per side, or until the tuna is cooked through and the vegetables are tender-crisp. Avoid overcooking the tuna.
7. Transfer the grilled tuna kabobs to serving plates. Squeeze fresh lemon juice over the kabobs (optional) and garnish with chopped fresh parsley for a touch of color.

NOTES

- **Tuna selection:** Choose fresh, firm tuna steaks for the best results.
- **Grilling pan alternative:** If you don't have a grill, you can cook the kabobs in a grill pan over medium heat on your stovetop.
- **Leftovers:** Leftover cooked tuna kabobs can be stored in an airtight container in the refrigerator for up to 2 days. Reheat gently on the stovetop or in the microwave until warmed through.

NUTRITIONAL INFORMATION (approximate per serving, without optional ingredients):
Calories: 350 | Protein: 30g | Fat: 15g | Carbohydrates: 20g | Sodium: 300mg (depending on sodium content of ingredients) | Potassium: 700mg (depending on ingredients)

Cherry-Chicken Lettuce Wraps with Lemon-Herb Yogurt Sauce

These vibrant cherry-chicken lettuce wraps are a perfect addition to the DASH diet. Packed with lean protein and wrapped in crisp lettuce leaves, they offer a satisfying and healthy low-carb meal. The flavorful chicken filling is balanced with a light and refreshing lemon-herb yogurt sauce, keeping sodium content in check.

Prep Time: 15 minutes || **Cook Time:** 15-20 minutes || **Yield:** 4 servings

INGREDIENTS

For the Chicken Filling:
- 1 pound boneless, skinless chicken breasts, thinly sliced
- 1 tablespoon olive oil
- ½ teaspoon dried thyme
- Pinch of garlic powder
- Pinch of freshly ground black pepper
- ¼ teaspoon ground ginger (optional)
- 1 cup chopped carrots
- 1 cup coarsely chopped pitted fresh sweet cherries
- ¼ cup chopped green onions

For the Lemon-Herb Yogurt Sauce:
- ½ cup plain low-fat Greek yogurt
- 1 tablespoon fresh lemon juice
- 1 tablespoon chopped fresh dill
- Pinch of dried oregano
- Pinch of freshly ground black pepper

For Serving:
- 16 large lettuce leaves (such as romaine or butter lettuce)
- ¼ cup chopped fresh parsley (optional)

INSTRUCTIONS

1. In a shallow dish, combine the sliced chicken breasts with olive oil, dried thyme, garlic powder, black pepper, and ground ginger (optional). Let the chicken marinate for 15 minutes (optional) to infuse flavor.
2. Heat olive oil in a large skillet over medium heat. Add the chicken (discarding the marinade if used) and cook for 5-7 minutes, or until golden brown and cooked through.
3. While the chicken cooks, add the chopped carrots to the skillet and cook for 2-3 minutes, or until slightly softened. Stir in the chopped cherries and green onions and cook for an additional minute or two.
4. In a small bowl, whisk together the plain low-fat Greek yogurt, fresh lemon juice, chopped fresh dill, dried oregano, and a pinch of black pepper.
5. Wash and dry the lettuce leaves. Place a spoonful of the chicken and vegetable mixture in each lettuce leaf. Drizzle with some lemon-herb yogurt sauce and garnish with chopped fresh parsley.
6. Enjoy the cherry-chicken lettuce wraps immediately while the lettuce leaves are crisp and the filling is warm.

NOTES
- **Chicken thickness:** Slice the chicken breasts thinly for even cooking.
- **Cherry variations:** Frozen cherries, thawed and drained, can be used instead of fresh cherries.
- **Herb variations:** Chopped fresh mint or chives can be used instead of dill in the sauce.

NUTRITIONAL INFORMATION (approximate per serving):
Calories: 300 | Protein: 30g | Fat: 10g | Carbohydrates: 20g | Sodium: 400mg (depending on sodium content of ingredients) | Potassium: 700mg (depending on ingredients)

Deconstructed Cabbage Roll Skillet with Light Tomato Broth

This flavorful deconstructed cabbage roll skillet offers a delicious and healthy twist on a classic dish, perfect for the DASH diet. Packed with ground turkey and brown rice, simmered in a light tomato broth with cabbage and spices, it delivers the satisfying taste of cabbage rolls without the need for stuffing leaves.

Prep Time: 15 minutes || **Cook Time:** 30-35 minutes || **Yield:** 4 servings

INGREDIENTS
For the Skillet:
- 1 tablespoon olive oil
- 1 pound lean ground turkey
- ½ medium yellow onion, chopped
- 1 carrot, diced
- 2 cloves garlic, minced
- ½ teaspoon dried thyme
- Pinch of dried oregano
- Pinch of ground cinnamon
- ¼ teaspoon crushed red pepper flakes (optional)
- 6 cups chopped green cabbage
- 1 (14.5-ounce) can diced tomatoes, undrained (fire-roasted or petite diced recommended)
- 1 ½ cups low-sodium chicken broth
- ½ cup cooked brown rice
- ½ cup chopped fresh parsley

INSTRUCTIONS
1. Heat the olive oil in a large skillet over medium heat.
2. Add the chopped onion and diced carrot to the hot skillet. Cook for 3-4 minutes, or until softened.
3. Add the ground turkey to the skillet and cook, breaking it up with a spoon, until browned. Drain any excess grease.
4. Stir in the minced garlic, dried thyme, dried oregano, ground cinnamon, and crushed red pepper flakes (optional). Cook for an additional minute, allowing the spices to release their aroma.
5. Add the chopped green cabbage and diced tomatoes (with their juices) to the skillet. Stir to combine.
6. Pour in the low-sodium chicken broth. Bring to a simmer, then reduce heat to low and cover the skillet. Simmer for 20-25 minutes, or until the cabbage is tender and cooked through.
7. Stir in the cooked brown rice and chopped fresh parsley. Cook for an additional 2-3 minutes, or until the rice is heated through.
8. Transfer the deconstructed cabbage roll skillet mixture to serving plates. Serve immediately with a sprinkle of additional chopped fresh parsley (optional).

NOTES
- **Ground meat variations:** You can substitute ground chicken or lean ground beef for the ground turkey in this recipe.
- **Brown rice alternatives:** Quinoa or another whole grain can be used instead of brown rice. Adjust the cooking time.
- **Cabbage variations:** You can use a combination of green cabbage and red cabbage for added color and flavor.

NUTRITIONAL INFORMATION (approximate per serving):
Calories: 400 | Protein: 30g | Fat: 15g | Carbohydrates: 35g | Sodium: 500mg (depending on sodium content of ingredients) | Potassium: 700mg (depending on ingredients)

Southwestern Brown Rice Bowl

This flavorful and satisfying southwestern brown rice bowl is a perfect lunch or dinner option for the DASH diet. Packed with protein-rich black beans, fiber-rich brown rice, and a variety of colorful vegetables, all seasoned with classic southwestern spices, it delivers a delicious and nutritious meal that keeps sodium in check.

Prep Time: 15 minutes || **Cook Time:** 40-45 minutes (depending on brown rice cooking time) || **Yield:** 2 servings

INGREDIENTS

For the Brown Rice:
- 1 cup uncooked brown rice
- 1 ½ cups low-sodium vegetable broth

For the Bowl:
- 1 tablespoon olive oil
- ½ cup chopped red bell pepper
- ½ cup chopped green bell pepper
- ½ cup chopped yellow onion
- 1 clove garlic, minced
- 1 (15-oz) can black beans, rinsed and drained
- 1 cup chopped corn (fresh or frozen)
- 1 Roma tomato, diced

- 1 jalapeño pepper, seeded and minced (optional, for a spicy kick)
- 1 teaspoon ground cumin
- ½ teaspoon chili powder
- ¼ teaspoon smoked paprika
- Pinch of garlic powder
- Pinch of black pepper
- ¼ cup chopped fresh cilantro
- Lime wedges (for serving)
- Optional toppings (choose from below):
  - Reduced-fat shredded cheese (cheddar or Monterey Jack)
  - Chopped avocado
  - Low-fat Greek yogurt
  - Salsa or pico de gallo

INSTRUCTIONS

1. In a medium saucepan, combine the uncooked brown rice and low-sodium vegetable broth. Bring to a boil, then reduce heat, cover, and simmer for 40-45 minutes, or until the rice is cooked through and fluffy. Once cooked, fluff the rice with a fork and set aside.
2. While the rice cooks, heat the olive oil in a large skillet or pan over medium heat. Add the chopped red bell pepper, green bell pepper, and yellow onion. Sauté for 5-7 minutes, or until softened.
3. Add the minced garlic, black beans, corn, diced tomato, jalapeño pepper (if using), ground cumin, chili powder, smoked paprika, garlic powder, and black pepper to the skillet with the softened vegetables. Stir to combine and cook for another 2-3 minutes, or until heated through.
4. Divide the cooked brown rice between two bowls. Top each bowl with the southwestern vegetable mixture. Garnish with chopped fresh cilantro and lime wedges.
5. Enjoy the southwestern brown rice bowl as is, or add your choice of optional toppings like reduced-fat shredded cheese, chopped avocado, low-fat Greek yogurt, salsa, or pico de gallo.

NOTES

- **Brown rice alternatives:** You can substitute pre-cooked brown rice for convenience, but cooking it yourself allows for more control over sodium content. Look for pre-cooked brown rice options labeled "low-sodium" or "no added salt."
- **Vegetable options:** Feel free to customize the vegetables based on your preferences. Other DASH-friendly options include chopped zucchini, poblano pepper, or chopped mushrooms.

- **Spiciness level:** Adjust the amount of jalapeño pepper to your desired level of spiciness. You can omit it entirely for a milder flavor.
- **Sodium content:** Be mindful of the sodium content in the black beans and choose a low-sodium canned variety whenever possible. Rinsing the beans can also help reduce some sodium content.

NUTRITIONAL INFORMATION (approximate per serving, without optional toppings):
Calories: 400 | Protein: 15g | Fat: 10g | Carbohydrates: 60g | Sodium: 400mg (depending on sodium content of ingredients) | Potassium: 700mg (depending on ingredients)

PART SIX

SNACKS & DESSERTS

Carrot Cake Cookies

These chewy and flavorful carrot cake cookies are a delicious and satisfying treat that fits perfectly with the DASH diet. They're made with whole-wheat flour, less sugar, and lower-sodium ingredients, keeping them healthy and enjoyable.

 **Prep Time:** 15 minutes || **Cook Time:** 12-15 minutes || **Yield:** 12-15 cookies

INGREDIENTS
- 1 ¾ cups whole-wheat flour
- 1 teaspoon baking soda
- 1 teaspoon ground cinnamon
- ½ teaspoon ground nutmeg
- ¼ teaspoon ground ginger
- ¼ teaspoon salt
- ½ cup unsalted butter, softened
- ½ cup granulated sugar substitute (such as stevia or erythritol)
- ¼ cup packed light brown sugar
- 1 large egg
- 1 teaspoon vanilla extract
- 1 cup grated carrots
- ½ cup chopped walnuts or pecans (optional)
- ½ cup raisins (optional)

INSTRUCTIONS
1. Preheat oven to 375°F (190°C) and line baking sheets with parchment paper.
2. In a medium bowl, whisk together the whole-wheat flour, baking soda, cinnamon, nutmeg, ginger, and salt.
3. In a large bowl, cream together the softened butter and sugar substitutes until light and fluffy. Beat in the brown sugar until well combined.
4. Add the egg and vanilla extract to the wet ingredients and mix until fully incorporated.
5. Gradually add the dry ingredients to the wet ingredients, mixing until just combined. Don't overmix.
6. Fold in the grated carrots and chopped nuts and raisins (if using).
7. Drop rounded tablespoons of dough onto the prepared baking sheets, leaving space between cookies for spreading.
8. Bake for 12-15 minutes, or until the edges are golden brown and the centers are slightly soft.
9. Let the cookies cool on the baking sheet for a few minutes before transferring them to a wire rack to cool completely.

NOTES
- For a vegan option, use a flaxseed egg instead of a regular egg. Mix 1 tablespoon of ground flaxseed with 3 tablespoons of water, let sit for 5 minutes until thickened, then use in place of the egg.
- You can substitute all-purpose flour for the whole-wheat flour, but the cookies will be slightly less nutritious.
- If the dough seems too dry, add 1 tablespoon of unsweetened applesauce at a time until it reaches a desired consistency.

NUTRITIONAL INFORMATION (approximate per cookie):
Calories: 200 | Protein: 2g | Fat: 8g | Carbohydrates: 30g | Sodium: 150mg (depending on sodium content of ingredients) | Potassium: 100mg (depending on ingredients)

Grilled Peaches with Greek Yogurt

This light and refreshing dessert is a perfect summer treat that fits the DASH diet. The sweetness of the grilled peaches complements the creamy Greek yogurt, while keeping sodium and added sugar in check.

Prep Time: 10 minutes || **Cook Time:** 10-12 minutes || **Yield:** 2 servings

INGREDIENTS
- 2 ripe peaches, halved and pitted
- 1 tablespoon olive oil
- ¼ cup low-fat plain Greek yogurt
- 1 tablespoon honey
- ½ teaspoon ground cinnamon
- Fresh mint leaves for garnish (optional)

INSTRUCTIONS
1. Preheat your grill to medium heat. You can also use a grill pan on your stovetop.
2. Brush the cut sides of the peaches with olive oil.
3. Place the peaches, cut side down, on the preheated grill. Grill for 4-5 minutes per side, or until softened and grill marks appear.
4. While the peaches are grilling, combine the Greek yogurt, honey, and cinnamon in a small bowl. Mix well.
5. Remove the peaches from the grill and place them cut side up on serving plates.
6. Spoon the yogurt mixture over the grilled peaches.
7. Garnish with fresh mint leaves (optional) and serve immediately.

NOTES
- Choose ripe but firm peaches for grilling. They will hold their shape better.
- If you don't have a grill or grill pan, you can broil the peaches in the oven for a few minutes until slightly softened and browned.
- For a vegan option, use plant-based yogurt instead of Greek yogurt.
- You can substitute maple syrup or agave nectar for honey.
- Experiment with different toppings suitable for the DASH diet. Chopped nuts, a sprinkle of granola, or a drizzle of low-fat vanilla yogurt can add extra flavor and texture.

NUTRITIONAL INFORMATION (approximate per serving):
Calories: 200 | Protein: 5g | Fat: 5g | Carbohydrates: 30g | Sodium: 60mg (depending on sodium content of yogurt) | Potassium: 250mg (depending on ingredients)

Dried Apricots and Almonds

Dried apricots and almonds are a portable and satisfying snack option that can be enjoyed on the DASH diet. This combination provides a good balance of nutrients and keeps sodium in check.

INGREDIENTS
- ¼ cup dried apricots, chopped
- ¼ cup raw almonds

INSTRUCTIONS
1. In a small bowl or reusable container, combine the chopped dried apricots and raw almonds.
2. Enjoy this snack mix as is, or portion it out into smaller containers for on-the-go convenience.

NOTES
- **Portion control:** This recipe provides a single serving size. Be mindful of portion sizes, especially with dried fruit, which can be higher in sugar.
- **Dried apricot selection:** Look for unsulfured dried apricots with no added sugar for a more natural option.
- **Almonds variety:** Raw almonds are a good choice, but roasted almonds without added salt can be used as well.
- **Alternative dried fruits:** Other DASH-friendly dried fruits like raisins, cranberries, or cherries can be substituted for the dried apricots, but be mindful of their sugar content.

Additional considerations:
- **Dried fruit and fiber:** While dried apricots offer some fiber, they are a concentrated source of sugar compared to fresh fruit.
- Soaking dried fruit (optional): Soaking dried apricots in warm water for 10 minutes can help plump them up and potentially reduce their glycemic index (GI) score, which can be helpful for blood sugar management.

NUTRITIONAL INFORMATION (approximate per serving):
Calories: 180 | Protein: 6g | Fat: 10g | Carbohydrates: 20g | Sodium: 20mg (depending on the sodium content of the dried apricots) | Potassium: 400mg (depending on ingredients)

Oil-Free White Bean Hummus

This creamy and flavorful hummus is a perfect addition to your DASH diet. Packed with protein and fiber from the white beans, it's naturally oil-free and lower in sodium, making it a healthy and satisfying dip.

**Prep Time:** 10 minutes || **Cook Time:** (depending on bean cooking method) || **Yield:** 2-3 servings

INGREDIENTS
- 1 (15 oz) can low-sodium cannellini beans, rinsed and drained
- ½ cup reserved bean cooking liquid (or low-sodium vegetable broth)
- 2 tablespoons tahini (optional, for a richer flavor)
- 2 tablespoons lemon juice
- 1 clove garlic, minced
- ½ teaspoon ground cumin
- ¼ teaspoon smoked paprika
- Pinch of cayenne pepper (optional)
- Salt and freshly ground black pepper to taste
- Fresh parsley or chives for garnish (optional)

INSTRUCTIONS
1. If using dried beans, cook them. Drain and reserve ½ cup of the cooking liquid. Canned beans can be used for a quicker option.
2. In a food processor or blender, combine the beans, reserved bean cooking liquid (or broth), tahini (if using), lemon juice, garlic, cumin, smoked paprika, and cayenne pepper (if using).
3. Pulse or blend until the hummus reaches a desired consistency. You may need to scrape down the sides occasionally for even blending.
4. Season with salt and black pepper to taste. Start with a small amount of salt and gradually add more to avoid over-salting.
5. Taste and adjust seasonings as needed. You can add a squeeze of additional lemon juice for a brighter flavor or a pinch of red pepper flakes for a touch of heat.
6. Transfer the hummus to a serving bowl. Garnish with a drizzle of olive oil (optional), fresh parsley or chives (optional), and a sprinkle of paprika.

NOTES
- For a smoother hummus, remove the skins from the beans before blending. You can do this by rubbing the cooked beans between your fingers after rinsing them.
- If the hummus is too thick, add more bean cooking liquid or water, one tablespoon at a time, until it reaches your desired consistency.
- Tahini is a sesame seed paste that adds a nutty flavor and creaminess to hummus. You can omit it for a completely oil-free option, but the texture will be slightly less rich.
- This hummus is delicious served with whole-wheat pita bread, carrot sticks, cucumber slices, or whole-grain crackers.
- Store leftover hummus in an airtight container in the refrigerator for up to 5 days.

NUTRITIONAL INFORMATION (approximate per serving, without optional tahini and olive oil):
Calories: 150 | Protein: 8g | Fat: 3g | Carbohydrates: 20g | Sodium: 200mg (depending on sodium content of ingredients) | Potassium: 400mg (depending on ingredients)

Herb Cream Cheese Stuffed Peppers

These colorful and flavorful bell peppers are a perfect appetizer or light lunch option for the DASH diet. They're filled with a creamy herb cream cheese mixture, low in sodium and packed with fresh flavors.

 **Prep Time:** 15 minutes || **Cook Time:** 30-35 minutes || **Yield:** 4 servings

INGREDIENTS
- 2 large bell peppers (red, yellow, orange, or a combination)
- 4 oz low-fat or fat-free cream cheese, softened
- ¼ cup chopped fresh herbs (such as parsley, chives, dill, or a combination)
- 2 tablespoons chopped red onion
- 1 clove garlic, minced
- ½ cup chopped mushrooms (optional)
- ¼ cup chopped cooked chicken breast or lentils (optional, for added protein)
- ¼ teaspoon dried oregano
- Pinch of freshly ground black pepper
- ¼ cup grated low-fat mozzarella cheese (optional)

INSTRUCTIONS
1. Preheat oven to 375°F (190°C). Wash the bell peppers and cut them in half lengthwise. Remove the seeds and membranes.
2. In a medium bowl, combine the softened cream cheese, chopped herbs, red onion, garlic, and chopped mushrooms (if using). Season with oregano and black pepper. Mix well until well combined.
3. If using chicken breast or lentils, fold them gently into the cream cheese mixture.
4. Stuff the bell pepper halves with the cream cheese mixture, dividing it evenly. You may not need all the filling depending on the size of the peppers.
5. Place the stuffed peppers in a baking dish. Pour about ¼ cup of water into the bottom of the dish to prevent burning.
6. Bake for 30-35 minutes, or until the peppers are tender and the filling is slightly golden brown on top.
7. If using mozzarella cheese, sprinkle it over the stuffed peppers in the last 5 minutes of baking for a melted cheesy topping (optional).
8. Let the peppers cool slightly before serving.

NOTES
- Look for pre-washed and chopped herbs to save time on prepping.
- Saute the chopped mushrooms in a pan with a teaspoon of water for a few minutes before adding them to the cream cheese mixture for extra flavor.
- You can substitute ricotta cheese for the cream cheese for a slightly lighter option.
- If you don't have fresh herbs, use 1 teaspoon of dried herbs of your choice.

NUTRITIONAL INFORMATION (approximate per serving, without optional chicken and mozzarella):
Calories: 200 | Protein: 8g | Fat: 5g | Carbohydrates: 25g | Sodium: 250mg (depending on sodium content of ingredients) | Potassium: 400mg (depending on ingredients)

Rainbow Slaw

This colorful and crunchy rainbow slaw is a perfect side dish for any DASH-friendly meal. Packed with vitamins and fiber from a variety of vegetables, it's low in sodium and bursting with fresh flavors.

 **Prep Time:** 10 minutes || **Cook Time:** N/A || **Yield:** 4-6 servings

INGREDIENTS
- 3 cups mixed shredded coleslaw (broccoli slaw, cabbage mix, etc.)
- 1 cup shredded carrots
- ½ cup chopped red bell pepper
- ½ cup chopped cucumber
- ¼ cup chopped red onion (optional)
- ¼ cup chopped fresh parsley
- 2 tablespoons olive oil
- 2 tablespoons lemon juice
- 1 tablespoon apple cider vinegar
- 1 teaspoon honey or pure maple syrup
- ½ teaspoon Dijon mustard
- ¼ teaspoon dried dill
- Salt and freshly ground black pepper to taste

INSTRUCTIONS
1. In a large bowl, combine the shredded coleslaw mix, carrots, red bell pepper, cucumber, and red onion (if using).
2. In a small bowl, whisk together the olive oil, lemon juice, apple cider vinegar, honey, Dijon mustard, and dried dill. Season with salt and pepper to taste.
3. Pour the dressing over the salad ingredients and toss gently until well coated.
4. Taste and adjust seasonings as needed. You may want to add a squeeze of additional lemon juice or a pinch of red pepper flakes for extra flavor.
5. Serve immediately or chill for at least 30 minutes for the flavors to develop. Garnish with fresh parsley before serving (optional).

NOTES
- Use pre-shredded vegetables to save time on prepping.
- You can experiment with different chopped vegetables suitable for the DASH diet. Chopped broccoli florets, cherry tomatoes, or shredded Brussels sprouts can be added for extra variety.
- If you prefer a creamier slaw, add 1-2 tablespoons of low-fat plain Greek yogurt to the dressing.
- For a vegan option, omit the honey and use a vegan mayonnaise or tahini-based dressing instead.
- Leftovers can be stored in an airtight container in the refrigerator for up to 3 days. The slaw may become slightly wilted, but will still be flavorful.

NUTRITIONAL INFORMATION (approximate per serving):
Calories: 150 | Protein: 1g | Fat: 5g | Carbohydrates: 20g | Sodium: 60mg (depending on sodium content of ingredients) | Potassium: 200mg (depending on ingredients)

Blueberry Muffins

These moist and delicious blueberry muffins are a perfect treat option for the DASH diet. They are packed with antioxidant-rich blueberries and use lower-sodium ingredients to keep you on track with your healthy eating goals.

Prep Time: 15 minutes || **Cook Time:** 20-25 minutes || **Yield:** 12 muffins

INGREDIENTS
- 1 ¾ cups whole wheat flour
- ½ cup rolled oats (not quick oats)
- 2 teaspoons baking powder
- ½ teaspoon baking soda
- ½ teaspoon ground cinnamon
- ¼ teaspoon ground nutmeg (optional)
- Pinch of salt
- 1 cup unsweetened almond milk (or low-fat dairy milk)
- ½ cup mashed ripe banana
- ¼ cup pure maple syrup
- 2 tablespoons canola oil
- 1 egg
- 1 cup fresh or frozen blueberries

INSTRUCTIONS
1. Preheat oven to 400°F (200°C). Line a muffin tin with paper liners or grease well with cooking spray.
2. In a large bowl, whisk together the dry ingredients: whole wheat flour, rolled oats, baking powder, baking soda, cinnamon, nutmeg (if using), and salt.
3. In a separate bowl, whisk together the almond milk (or dairy milk), mashed banana, maple syrup, canola oil, and egg.
4. Pour the wet ingredients into the dry ingredients and stir gently until just combined. Be careful not to overmix, as this can lead to tough muffins. Fold in the blueberries.
5. Divide the batter evenly among the prepared muffin cups. The batter will be thick.
6. Bake the muffins for 20-25 minutes, or until a toothpick inserted into the center comes out clean.
7. Let the muffins cool in the pan for a few minutes before transferring them to a wire rack to cool completely.

NOTES
- Use ripe bananas for the best sweetness and flavor.
- If the batter seems too thick, add a tablespoon or two of additional almond milk (or dairy milk) until it reaches a pourable consistency.
- Tossing the blueberries in a little bit of flour before adding them to the batter can help prevent them from sinking to the bottom of the muffins.
- For a vegan option, use a flaxseed egg instead of a regular egg (see instructions above in Banana Oatmeal Pancakes recipe).
- You can experiment with different DASH-friendly toppings or additions:
  - A sprinkle of chopped nuts (almonds, walnuts) before baking
  - A dollop of low-fat plain Greek yogurt with a drizzle of honey after baking

NUTRITIONAL INFORMATION (approximate per serving):
Calories: 250 | Protein: 5g | Fat: 8g | Carbohydrates: 40g | Sodium: 180mg (depending on sodium content of ingredients) | Potassium: 200mg (depending on ingredients)

Spicy Almonds

These crunchy and flavorful spicy almonds are a perfect on-the-go snack option for the DASH diet. Packed with protein and healthy fats from the almonds, and a delicious low-sodium spice blend, they satisfy your cravings while keeping sodium in check.

Prep Time: 10 minutes || **Cook Time:** 15-20 minutes || **Yield:** 4-6 servings

INGREDIENTS
- 1 cup raw almonds
- 1 tablespoon olive oil
- ½ teaspoon chili powder
- ¼ teaspoon smoked paprika
- ¼ teaspoon ground cumin
- Pinch of cayenne pepper (optional, for extra spice)
- Pinch of garlic powder
- Pinch of black pepper
- ¼ teaspoon sea salt (or to taste, depending on desired sodium level)

INSTRUCTIONS
1. Preheat your oven to 300°F (150°C).
2. In a medium bowl, toss the raw almonds with the olive oil. Make sure the almonds are evenly coated.
3. In a small bowl, combine the chili powder, smoked paprika, ground cumin, cayenne pepper (if using), garlic powder, and black pepper. Add this spice blend to the bowl with the olive oil-coated almonds and toss again to ensure all the almonds are coated evenly.
4. Spread the seasoned almonds on a baking sheet in a single layer. Bake for 15-20 minutes, stirring occasionally, or until the almonds are golden brown and fragrant.
5. Once the almonds are toasted, remove them from the oven and sprinkle with the sea salt (or to taste). Let the almonds cool completely on the baking sheet before transferring them to an airtight container.

NOTES
- **Adjust the spice level:** This recipe offers a mild-medium spice level. You can adjust the amount of cayenne pepper to suit your preference.
- **Alternative spices:** Feel free to experiment with other DASH-friendly spices like dried oregano, thyme, or rosemary.
- **Non-stick baking sheet:** Using a non-stick baking sheet can help prevent the almonds from sticking during cooking.
- **Storage:** Store the cooled spicy almonds in an airtight container at room temperature for up to a week.

NUTRITIONAL INFORMATION (approximate per serving):
Calories: 180 | Protein: 6g | Fat: 14g | Carbohydrates: 6g | Sodium: 80mg (depending on amount of salt used) | Potassium: 130mg (depending on ingredients)

Blueberry Banana Spelt Muffins

These delicious and wholesome muffins are a perfect DASH-friendly breakfast or snack. Packed with fiber-rich spelt flour, potassium-rich bananas, and antioxidants from blueberries, they offer a satisfying and nutritious start to your day. This recipe keeps sodium in check by using low-sodium ingredients and natural sweetness from the fruit.

Prep Time: 10 minutes || **Cook Time:** 20-25 minutes || **Yield:** 6 muffins

INGREDIENTS

For the Muffins:
- 1 ½ cups whole spelt flour
- 1 teaspoon baking powder
- ½ teaspoon baking soda
- ½ teaspoon ground cinnamon
- ¼ teaspoon ground nutmeg (optional)
- Pinch of salt
- 1 ripe banana, mashed
- ½ cup unsweetened applesauce
- ¼ cup low-fat milk (or unsweetened plant-based milk alternative)
- 1 tablespoon honey (or maple syrup)
- 1 egg, beaten
- 1 cup fresh or frozen blueberries

INSTRUCTIONS

1. Preheat your oven to 400°F (200°C). Grease a muffin tin or line it with paper muffin liners for easier cleanup.
2. In a large bowl, whisk together the whole spelt flour, baking powder, baking soda, ground cinnamon, ground nutmeg (if using), and salt.
3. In a separate bowl, mash the ripe banana and whisk it together with the unsweetened applesauce, low-fat milk, honey (or maple syrup), and beaten egg.
4. Pour the wet ingredients into the dry ingredients and stir gently with a spatula until just combined. Be careful not to overmix.
5. Gently fold in the fresh or frozen blueberries using a rubber spatula. Avoid overmixing to prevent the blueberries from bursting.
6. Divide the batter evenly among the prepared muffin cups.
7. Bake the muffins in the preheated oven for 20-25 minutes, or until a toothpick inserted into the center of a muffin comes out clean.
8. Let the muffins cool in the muffin tin for a few minutes before transferring them to a wire rack to cool completely. Enjoy them warm or at room temperature.

NOTES

- **Spelt flour:** Spelt flour is a good source of fiber and adds a slightly nutty flavor to the muffins. You can substitute whole wheat flour for spelt flour if needed.
- **Honey or maple syrup:** A touch of honey or maple syrup adds sweetness to the muffins. You can adjust the amount based on your preference or omit it entirely for a naturally sweetened option.
- **Milk options:** Low-fat milk or unsweetened plant-based milk alternatives like almond milk or oat milk can be used.
- **Fresh vs. frozen blueberries:** Both fresh and frozen blueberries work well in this recipe. If using frozen blueberries, you don't need to thaw them beforehand, but they might take a few minutes longer to bake.

NUTRITIONAL INFORMATION (approximate per muffin):
Calories: 250 | Protein: 5g | Fat: 5g | Carbohydrates: 40g | Sodium: 150mg (depending on sodium content of ingredients) | Potassium: 200mg (depending on ingredients)

Clementine and Sunflower Seed Snack

This refreshing and satisfying combination of clementines and sunflower seeds is a perfect snack option for the DASH diet. Packed with vitamin C from the clementines and healthy fats and protein from the sunflower seeds, it delivers a delicious and nutritious snack that keeps sodium in check.

INGREDIENTS
- 1 clementine
- ¼ cup raw sunflower seeds

INSTRUCTIONS
1. Peel the clementine, separating it into individual segments.
2. Enjoy the clementine segments and sunflower seeds together. You can eat them alternately or mix them in a small bowl.

NOTES
- **Portion control:** This recipe provides a single serving size. Be mindful of portion sizes, especially with sunflower seeds, as they are higher in calories.
- **Clementine variations:** You can substitute other citrus fruits like tangerines or cuties for the clementine.
- **Sunflower seed options:** Raw sunflower seeds are a good choice, but roasted sunflower seeds without added salt can be used as well.

Additional considerations:
- **Sugar content:** Clementines are a naturally sweet fruit, but they are also a good source of vitamin C and fiber.
- **Sunflower seeds and healthy fats:** Sunflower seeds are a good source of healthy fats, including polyunsaturated fats, which can help improve heart health.

NUTRITIONAL INFORMATION (approximate per serving):
Calories: 160 | Protein: 5g | Fat: 10g | Carbohydrates: 15g | Sodium: 15mg (depending on sodium content of ingredients) | Potassium: 200mg (depending on ingredients)

Chickpea Brownies

These delectable chickpea brownies offer a delicious and satisfying treat option for the DASH diet. Packed with protein and fiber-rich chickpeas, natural sweetness from dates, and a touch of cocoa powder for rich chocolatey flavor, they deliver a healthier alternative to traditional brownies while keeping sodium in check.

 **Prep Time:** 15 minutes || **Cook Time:** 20-25 minutes || **Yield:** 8-10 brownies

INGREDIENTS
- 1 can (15 oz) chickpeas, drained and rinsed
- ½ cup pitted Medjool dates
- ¼ cup unsweetened almond milk (or other low-sugar plant-based milk)
- ¼ cup unsweetened cocoa powder
- 2 tablespoons natural peanut butter (creamy, unsweetened)
- 1 tablespoon melted coconut oil (or unsalted butter)
- 1 teaspoon vanilla extract
- ½ teaspoon ground cinnamon
- ¼ teaspoon baking powder
- Pinch of salt

INSTRUCTIONS
1. Preheat your oven to 350°F (175°C). Line an 8x8 inch baking pan with parchment paper for easy removal.
2. In a food processor or high-powered blender, combine the drained and rinsed chickpeas, pitted Medjool dates, unsweetened almond milk, cocoa powder, peanut butter, melted coconut oil (or butter), vanilla extract, ground cinnamon, baking powder, and salt. Blend until smooth and creamy, scraping down the sides as needed.
3. Pour the batter into the prepared baking pan and spread evenly. Bake for 20-25 minutes, or until a toothpick inserted into the center comes out with moist crumbs (not completely clean).
4. Let the brownies cool completely in the pan before cutting and serving. This allows them to firm up properly. You can chill them in the refrigerator for an extra fudgy texture (optional).

NOTES
- **Sweetener options:** Medjool dates provide natural sweetness, but you can adjust the quantity based on their sweetness level. Alternatively, a drizzle of maple syrup or honey can be added after blending for additional sweetness, but use them sparingly.
- **Nut butter selection:** Choose a natural peanut butter with no added sugar or salt for a lower-sodium option. Other nut butters like almond butter or cashew butter can be used as well.
- **Fat source:** Melted coconut oil is a good option for a dairy-free and potentially lower-sodium alternative to butter.
- **Serving suggestions:** Enjoy the brownies plain, or top them with a sprinkle of chopped nuts, a dollop of low-fat Greek yogurt, or a drizzle of melted dark chocolate (look for options with at least 70% cacao for lower sugar content).

NUTRITIONAL INFORMATION (approximate per brownie):
Calories: 180 | Protein: 5g | Fat: 8g (depending on fat source) | Carbohydrates: 25g | Sodium: 70mg (depending on sodium content of ingredients) | Potassium: 200mg (depending on ingredients)

Skinny Quinoa Veggie Dip with Lemon and Herbs

This vibrant and flavorful dip is a perfect party appetizer or healthy snack option that fits perfectly into the DASH diet. Packed with protein and fiber from quinoa, this recipe keeps sodium content in check and uses fresh ingredients for a delicious and nutritious dip.

**Prep Time:** 15 minutes || **Cook Time:** 15 minutes (for quinoa) || **Yield:** About 2 cups

INGREDIENTS

For the Quinoa:
- ½ cup rinsed quinoa
- 1 cup low-sodium vegetable broth

For the Dip:
- 1 cup roasted red bell pepper (jarred or roasted fresh)
- ½ cup chopped cucumber
- ½ cup chopped cherry tomatoes
- ¼ cup crumbled low-fat feta cheese (optional)
- ¼ cup chopped fresh parsley
- 2 tablespoons chopped fresh chives
- 1 tablespoon lemon juice
- 1 tablespoon olive oil
- Pinch of garlic powder
- Pinch of salt and freshly ground black pepper (optional)

INSTRUCTIONS

1. In a saucepan, combine the rinsed quinoa and low-sodium vegetable broth. Bring to a boil, then reduce heat to low, cover, and simmer for 15 minutes, or until the quinoa is cooked through and fluffy. Fluff the quinoa with a fork and let it cool slightly.
2. If using a jarred roasted red bell pepper, drain any excess liquid. Chop the cucumber and cherry tomatoes. Crumble the low-fat feta cheese (optional). Chop the fresh parsley and chives.
3. In a large bowl, combine the cooked quinoa, roasted red bell pepper, chopped cucumber, cherry tomatoes, crumbled feta cheese (optional), chopped fresh parsley, and chopped fresh chives.
4. In a small bowl, whisk together lemon juice, olive oil, garlic powder, and a pinch of salt and freshly ground black pepper (optional).
5. Pour the dressing over the quinoa and vegetable mixture. Stir gently to coat everything evenly.
6. Serve the dip immediately with your favorite crudités like sliced carrots, celery sticks, bell pepper strips, or whole-wheat pita bread.

NOTES

- **Roasting red peppers:** You can roast a fresh red bell pepper yourself by placing it on a baking sheet under a broiler until blackened on the skin. Then, place the pepper in a paper bag for 15 minutes to steam. Remove the skin and chop the pepper.
- **Feta cheese:** Crumbled low-fat feta cheese adds a salty element, but you can omit it for a completely vegan option.
- **Leftovers:** Leftover dip can be stored in an airtight container in the refrigerator for up to 2 days.
- **Flavor variations:** Experiment with different herbs like dill, mint, or oregano for a variety of flavors.

NUTRITIONAL INFORMATION (approximate per serving, without feta cheese):
Calories: 200 | Protein: 5g | Fat: 5g | Carbohydrates: 30g | Sodium: 150mg (depending on sodium content of ingredients) | Potassium: 400mg (depending on ingredients)

Mango Rice Pudding with Coconut Milk and Almonds

This vibrant mango rice pudding offers a delicious and healthy dessert option for the DASH diet. Creamy rice pudding cooked in coconut milk is bursting with the sweetness of fresh mangoes and the nutty crunch of toasted almonds. This recipe keeps sodium content in check by using low-sodium ingredients and natural flavors.

Prep Time: 15 minutes || **Cook Time:** 30-35 minutes || **Yield:** 4 servings

INGREDIENTS

For the Rice Pudding:
- ½ cup brown rice (rinsed)
- 2 cups unsweetened low-fat coconut milk
- 1 cup low-sodium milk
- ¼ cup granulated sugar (or substitute with a natural sweetener like maple syrup or monk fruit sweetener)
- 1 teaspoon vanilla extract
- Pinch of ground cinnamon
- Pinch of salt (optional)

For the Mango Topping:
- 1 ripe mango, diced
- 2 tablespoons sliced almonds, toasted

INSTRUCTIONS

1. In a medium saucepan, combine the rinsed brown rice, unsweetened low-fat coconut milk, low-sodium milk, granulated sugar (or substitute), vanilla extract, ground cinnamon, and a pinch of salt (optional).
2. Bring the mixture to a boil over medium heat. Reduce heat, cover the pan, and simmer for 30-35 minutes, or until the rice is cooked through and the pudding thickens. Stir occasionally to prevent sticking.
3. While the rice pudding cooks, dice the ripe mango. Toast the sliced almonds in a dry skillet over medium heat until fragrant and golden brown, watching closely to avoid burning.
4. Once the rice pudding is cooked, remove it from the heat. Divide the warm pudding among serving bowls. Top each serving with diced fresh mango and toasted almonds.
5. Enjoy the mango rice pudding warm or chilled. Leftovers can be stored in the refrigerator for up to 3 days.

NOTES
- **Brown rice alternatives**: You can substitute white rice for brown rice, but brown rice offers additional fiber. Adjust the cooking time slightly for white rice, following package **INSTRUCTIONS**.
- **Mango variations:** Frozen diced mango can be used instead of fresh mango. Thaw and drain the frozen mango before adding it to the rice pudding.
- **Sweetener variations:** Adjust the amount of sweetener to your taste preference. You can also use a combination of granulated sugar and another natural sweetener like maple syrup or monk fruit sweetener.
- **Leftovers:** Leftover rice pudding can be stored in an airtight container in the refrigerator for up to 3 days. The texture may thicken as it cools, so you can add a splash of low-sodium milk when reheating to achieve the desired consistency.

NUTRITIONAL INFORMATION (approximate per serving):
Calories: 350 | Protein: 5g | Fat: 15g | Carbohydrates: 40g | Sodium: 250mg (depending on sodium content of ingredients) | Potassium: 400mg (depending on ingredients)

Cannellini Bean Hummus with Roasted Garlic and Lemon Zest

This flavorful hummus recipe is a perfect addition to the DASH diet. Made with cannellini beans, it offers a creamy and protein-packed dip while keeping sodium content in check. Roasted garlic adds a touch of sweetness, and a hint of lemon zest brightens the flavor profile.

 **Prep Time:** 15 minutes || **Cook Time:** 30 minutes (for roasting garlic) ||  **Yield:** About 2 cups

INGREDIENTS

For the Roasted Garlic:
- 1 head garlic (whole)
- Olive oil

For the Hummus:
- 1 (15 oz) can cannellini beans, rinsed and drained
- ¼ cup tahini (or olive oil)
- 2 tablespoons fresh lemon juice
- 2 tablespoons olive oil
- 1 clove roasted garlic (from the head above)
- ¼ cup water (add more gradually as needed)
- ½ teaspoon ground cumin
- Pinch of salt and freshly ground black pepper (optional)
- 1 tablespoon chopped fresh parsley (for garnish)
- Lemon zest (from 1 lemon, for garnish)

INSTRUCTIONS

1. Preheat your oven to 400°F (200°C). Cut off the top 1/4 inch of the head of garlic to expose the cloves. Drizzle the garlic head with olive oil and wrap it loosely in aluminum foil. Roast in the preheated oven for 30 minutes, or until the cloves are soft and golden brown. Let cool slightly.
2. In a food processor or blender, combine the rinsed and drained cannellini beans, tahini (or olive oil), fresh lemon juice, olive oil, roasted garlic clove (squeezed from the roasted head), ground cumin, and a pinch of salt and freshly ground black pepper (optional).
3. Process the ingredients until the hummus reaches a desired consistency, scraping down the sides as needed. Gradually add water, one tablespoon at a time, until the hummus is smooth and creamy.
4. Taste the hummus and adjust seasonings with additional lemon juice, salt, or pepper if desired.
5. Transfer the hummus to a serving bowl. Drizzle with a little olive oil and sprinkle with chopped fresh parsley and lemon zest for garnish. Serve with pita bread, cut vegetables, or whole-wheat crackers for dipping.

NOTES

- **Tahini substitution:** If you don't have tahini, you can substitute it with an equal amount of olive oil. The tahini adds a richer flavor and texture, but the hummus will still be delicious without it.
- **Water adjustment:** The amount of water needed will depend on the desired consistency of your hummus. Start with less and add more gradually until you reach a smooth and creamy texture.
- Leftovers: Store leftover hummus in an airtight container in the refrigerator for up to 5 days.

NUTRITIONAL INFORMATION (approximate per serving, without garnish):
Calories: 150 | Protein: 5g | Fat: 8g | Carbohydrates: 20g | Sodium: 300mg (depending on sodium content of ingredients) | Potassium: 500mg (depending on ingredients)

Raspberry Peach Puff Pancake with Lemon-Ricotta Sauce

This vibrant raspberry peach puff pancake offers a delightful and healthy dessert option for the DASH diet. Light and fluffy with fresh fruit, it's drizzled with a flavorful lemon-ricotta sauce that keeps sodium content in check while boasting a refreshing citrusy taste.

 **Prep Time:** 15 minutes || **Cook Time:** 20-25 minutes || **Yield:** 4 servings

INGREDIENTS

For the Puff Pancake:
- 2 large eggs, separated
- ¼ cup low-fat milk
- ¼ cup unsweetened almond milk (or low-fat milk)
- ¼ cup whole wheat pastry flour
- Pinch of ground cinnamon
- Pinch of salt (optional)
- 1 tablespoon olive oil
- 1 peach, thinly sliced

- ½ cup fresh raspberries

For the Lemon-Ricotta Sauce:
- ½ cup low-fat ricotta cheese
- 1 tablespoon fresh lemon juice
- 1 tablespoon powdered sugar (or substitute with a natural sweetener like maple syrup or monk fruit sweetener)
- Pinch of ground cinnamon

INSTRUCTIONS

1. Preheat your oven to 400°F (200°C). Lightly grease a 10-inch oven-safe skillet or baking dish.
2. Separate the egg whites from the yolks in two separate bowls.
3. In a medium bowl, whisk together the egg yolks, low-fat milk, unsweetened almond milk (or milk), whole wheat pastry flour, ground cinnamon, and a pinch of salt (optional) until smooth.
4. In a clean bowl, use a hand mixer or whisk to beat the egg whites until stiff peaks form.
5. Gently fold the beaten egg whites into the egg yolk mixture using a spatula. Be careful not to deflate the egg whites.
6. Heat the olive oil in the preheated oven-safe skillet over medium heat.
7. Pour the batter into the hot skillet and swirl it gently to spread evenly.
8. Top the batter with the sliced peaches and fresh raspberries.
9. Bake the puff pancake in the preheated oven for 20-25 minutes, or until the center is puffed and golden brown.
10. While the pancake bakes, in a small bowl, whisk together the low-fat ricotta cheese, fresh lemon juice, powdered sugar (or substitute), and a pinch of ground cinnamon until smooth.
11. Once the puff pancake is golden brown and cooked through, remove it from the oven. Let it cool slightly on a wire rack for a few minutes. Slice the pancake into wedges and serve warm on plates. Drizzle each serving with the lemon-ricotta sauce (optional) and enjoy!

NOTES

- **Sweetener variations:** Adjust the amount of powdered sugar (or substitute) to your taste preference. You can also use a combination of powdered sugar and another natural sweetener like maple syrup or monk fruit sweetener.
- **Serving variations:** For an extra touch, serve the puff pancake with a dollop of low-fat whipped cream or a scoop of low-sugar vanilla ice cream.

NUTRITIONAL INFORMATION (approximate per serving):

Calories: 250 | Protein: 10g | Fat: 10g | Carbohydrates: 30g | Sodium: 200mg (depending on sodium content of ingredients) | Potassium: 300mg (depending on ingredients)

Fruit and Almond Bites with Optional Yogurt Drizzle

These no-bake fruit and almond bites packed with protein-rich almonds, dried fruit, and rolled oats, they are naturally sweetened and free of added sugars. This recipe keeps sodium content in check while boasting a delightful combination of textures and flavors.

 Prep Time: 10 minutes || **Chill Time:** 30 minutes (or up to overnight) ||  **Yield:** 12 bites

INGREDIENTS
- ½ cup rolled oats (old-fashioned or quick oats)
- ½ cup chopped almonds
- ¼ cup unsweetened shredded coconut (optional)
- ¼ cup chopped dried fruits (such as dates, raisins, cranberries, or a mix)

- 2 tablespoons almond butter (or other nut butter like peanut butter or cashew butter)
- 1 tablespoon honey (or maple syrup)
- 1 tablespoon unsweetened applesauce

Optional Yogurt Drizzle:
- ¼ cup plain low-fat Greek yogurt
- 1 teaspoon honey (or maple syrup)

INSTRUCTIONS
1. In a large bowl, combine the rolled oats, chopped almonds, unsweetened shredded coconut (optional), and chopped dried fruits.
2. In a separate small bowl, whisk together the almond butter (or nut butter), honey (or maple syrup), and unsweetened applesauce until well combined.
3. Add the wet ingredients to the dry ingredient mixture in the bowl. Stir together until everything is well coated and the mixture holds its shape when squeezed.
4. Using a spoon or your hands, scoop out the mixture and roll it into balls to form bite-sized pieces. Place the formed bites on a baking sheet lined with parchment paper.
5. Refrigerate the baking sheet with the fruit and almond bites for at least 30 minutes, or up to overnight, to allow them to firm up.
6. In a small bowl, whisk together the plain low-fat Greek yogurt and honey (or maple syrup) until smooth.
7. Once chilled, remove the fruit and almond bites from the refrigerator. Drizzle them with the optional yogurt drizzle if desired. Enjoy these healthy and delicious bites as a snack or a quick breakfast on the go.

NOTES
- **Dried fruit variations:** You can use a variety of chopped dried fruits according to your preference. Just be mindful of moisture content – very moist fruits may require slightly less applesauce in the recipe.
- **Nut butter variations:** Substitute the almond butter with another nut butter you enjoy, like peanut butter or cashew butter.
- **Sweetener variations:** If you prefer a sweeter taste, add an extra teaspoon of honey or maple syrup to the wet ingredients mixture. You can also use a natural sweetener like monk fruit sweetener.

NUTRITIONAL INFORMATION (approximate per serving, without yogurt drizzle):
Calories: 180 | Protein: 5g | Fat: 10g | Carbohydrates: 20g | Sodium: 30mg (depending on sodium content of ingredients) | Potassium: 100mg (depending on ingredients)

PART SEVEN

MEAL PLAN

Meal Plans (1200, 1400, and 1600 Calories)

Daily meals will follow the DASH eating plan guidelines for servings from each food group.

1200 CALORIES MEAL PLAN

DAYS	BREAFAST	LUNCH	DINNER	SNACKS
DAY 1	Banana Chia Overnight Oats (B) with 1/4 cup berries	Black Bean Salad (S&S) with 1 whole-wheat pita bread and 1 tablespoon light vinaigrette	Lemon-Garlic Shrimp Over Orzo with Zucchini (L&D)	Dried Apricots and Almonds (S)
DAY 2	Pumpkin Yogurt Parfait with Granola (B)	Veggie and Hummus Sandwich (L) on whole-wheat bread with lettuce and tomato	Curried Cauliflower Steaks with Red Rice & Tzatziki (L&D)	Clementine and Sunflower Seed Snack (S)
DAY 3	Muesli Scones (B) with 1/4 cup low-fat yogurt and berries	Shrimp and Nectarine Salad with Lemon Herb Vinaigrette (L)	Southwest Tofu Scramble (D) with a side salad	Skinny Quinoa Veggie Dip with Lemon and Herbs (S) with baby carrots
DAY 4	Raspberry Yogurt Cereal Bowl (B) with 1 cup whole-wheat flakes and 1/4 cup berries	: Turkish Red Lentil Soup (Kırmızı Mercimek Çorbası) (S&L) with 1 slice whole-wheat bread	Hasselback Eggplant Parmesan (D) with a side of marinara sauce for dipping	Fruit and Almond Bites with Optional Yogurt Drizzle (S)
DAY 5	Herbed Wild Mushroom Oatmeal with Flaxseed Meal (B)	Warm Rice and Pintos Salad with Light Vinaigrette and Fresh Herbs (L)	Peppered Sole with Lemon and Herbs (D) with roasted asparagus	Oil-Free White Bean Hummus (S) with baby carrots
DAY 6	Low-Sodium Waffles (B) with 1/4 cup berries and 1 tablespoon light yogurt	Chicken and Vegetable Penne with Parsley-Walnut Pesto (L)	:Black Bean and Sweet Potato Rice Bowls with Cilantro Lime Vinaigrette (D)	Spicy Almonds (S)
DAY 7	Eggplant Florentine with Light Cream Sauce and Spinach (B) with 1 slice whole-wheat toast	Mediterranean Quinoa Bowls with Roasted Red Pepper Sauce (L)	Deconstructed Cabbage Roll Skillet with Light Tomato Broth (D)	Grilled Peaches with Greek Yogurt (S)

1400 CALORIE MEAL PLAN

DAYS	BREAKFAST	LUNCH	DINNER	SNACKS
DAY 1	Sweet Potato Oat Waffles (B) with 1/2 cup berries and 1/4 cup low-fat yogurt	Black Bean Salad (S&S) with 2 whole-wheat pita bread and 2 tablespoons light vinaigrette	Sesame Ginger Chicken with Cauliflower Rice (L&D) with a side salad	Clementine and Sunflower Seed Snack (S) and a handful of mixed nuts
DAY 2	Banana Oatmeal Pancakes (B) with 1/4 cup berries and 1 tablespoon maple syrup	Veggie Quesadillas with Cilantro Yogurt Dip (L) on whole-wheat tortillas with mixed greens	Chickpea and Potato Curry with Spinach (L&D) with 1 cup brown rice	Clementine and Sunflower Seed Snack (S) and a handful of mixed nuts
DAY 3	Blueberry Yogurt Multigrain Pancakes (B) with 1/4 cup berries and 1 tablespoon maple syrup	Shrimp and Nectarine Salad with Lemon Herb Vinaigrette (L) with 1 cup quinoa	Three Bean Chili with Vegetables and Spices (D) with a side salad	Skinny Quinoa Veggie Dip with Lemon and Herbs (S) with baby carrots and sugar snap peas

DAY 4	Ezekiel Bread French Toast with Berries and Nut Butter (B) with 1 slice Ezekiel bread	Turkish Red Lentil Soup (Kırmızı Mercimek Çorbası) (S&L) with 1 slice whole-wheat bread and 1 ounce low-fat cheese	Walnut-Rosemary Crusted Salmon (D) with roasted Brussels sprouts	Fruit and Almond Bites with Optional Yogurt Drizzle (S) and a pear
DAY 5	Yogurt Parfait with Berries, Granola, and Chia Seeds (B) with 1/2 cup granola and 1/4 cup berries	Warm Rice and Pintos Salad with Light Vinaigrette and Fresh Herbs (L) with 1 ounce grilled chicken or fish	Chicken Souvlaki with Herbed Couscous (L&D) with a side of grilled vegetables	Oil-Free White Bean Hummus (S) with cucumber slices and whole-wheat crackers
DAY 6	Banana Chia Overnight Oats (B) with 1/2 cup berries and 1/4 cup chopped nuts	Chicken and Vegetable Penne with Parsley-Walnut Pesto (L) with a side salad	Sweet Potato and Black Bean Tacos (D) on whole-wheat tortillas with all the fixings (lettuce, tomato, salsa, avocado	Spicy Almonds (S) and a cup of green tea
DAY 7	Mushroom Spinach Omelet with Herbs (B) with 1 slice whole-wheat toast	Mediterranean Quinoa Bowls with Roasted Red Pepper Sauce (L) with grilled chicken breast	Portobello Florentine with Light Cream Sauce and Spinach (D) with 1 cup quinoa	Grilled Peaches with Greek Yogurt (S) and a sprinkle of granola

1600 CALORIE MEAL PLAN

DAYS	BREAKFAST	LUNCH	DINNER	SNACKS
DAY 1	Blueberry Yogurt Multigrain Pancakes (B) with 1/2 cup berries and 1/4 cup maple syrup	Black Bean Salad (S&S) with 2 whole-wheat pita bread, 2 tablespoons light vinaigrette, and 1 ounce low-fat cheese	Sesame Chicken (L&D) with 1 cup brown rice and a side salad	Dried Apricots and Almonds (S) and 1 cup low-fat Greek yogurt
DAY 2	Banana Oatmeal Pancakes (B) with 1/2 cup berries and 1/4 cup maple syrup	Chickpea Pasta with Mushrooms, Kale, and Cherry Tomatoes (L) with 1 cup whole-wheat bread	Lemon-Herb Salmon with Caponata and Farro (L&D)	Clementine and Sunflower Seed Snack (S) and a handful of trail mix
DAY 3	Muesli Scones (B) with 1/2 cup low-fat yogurt and 1/4 cup berries	Quinoa and Vegetable Stew (S&L) with 1 ounce grilled chicken or fish	Spinach-Stuffed Turkey Burger Patties with Avocado Crema (D) on a whole-wheat bun with lettuce, tomato, and onion	Skinny Quinoa Veggie Dip with Lemon and Herbs (S) with baby carrots, sugar snap peas, and whole-wheat crackers
DAY 4	Eggplant Florentine with Light Cream Sauce and Spinach (B) with 2 slices whole-wheat toast	Turkish Red Lentil Soup (Kırmızı Mercimek Çorbası) (S&L) with 2 slices whole-wheat bread and 1 ounce low-fat cheese	Beef and Butternut Squash Penne with Pesto (L&D) with a side salad	Fruit and Almond Bites with Optional Yogurt Drizzle (S) and a banana
DAY 5	Yogurt Parfait with Berries, Granola, and Chia Seeds (B) with 1 cup granola and 1/2 cup berries	Warm Rice and Pintos Salad with Light Vinaigrette and Fresh Herbs (L) with 3 ounces grilled chicken or fish	Deconstructed Cabbage Roll Skillet with Light Tomato Broth (D) with 1 cup quinoa and grilled chicken breast	Oil-Free White Bean Hummus (S) with whole-wheat pita bread and vegetable sticks
DAY 6	Sweet Potato Oat Waffles (B) with 1/2 cup berries, 1/4 cup chopped nuts,	Chicken and Vegetable Penne with Parsley-Walnut Pesto (L) with a	Shrimp Orzo with Lemon-Herb Feta (L&D) with 1 cup whole-wheat	Spicy Almonds (S) and a cup of berries

		side salad and 1 ounce low-fat cheese	bread	
	and 1 tablespoon maple syrup			
DAY7	Mushroom Spinach Omelet with Herbs (B) with 2 slices whole-wheat toast and 1 sausage link	Mediterranean Quinoa Bowls with Roasted Red Pepper Sauce (L) with grilled salmon	California Quinoa with Light Vinaigrette and Fresh Herbs (D) with grilled chicken breast	Grilled Peaches with Greek Yogurt (S) and a sprinkle of granola and chopped nuts

Important Note: These are samples and portion sizes may need to be adjusted based on individual needs. It's recommended to consult a healthcare professional or registered dietitian for personalized meal plans.

KEY
B = Breakfast **L** = Lunch **D** = Dinner **S** = Snack

PART EIGHT

CONVERSION GUIDE & MEAL PLANNERS

KITCHEN CONVERSIONS

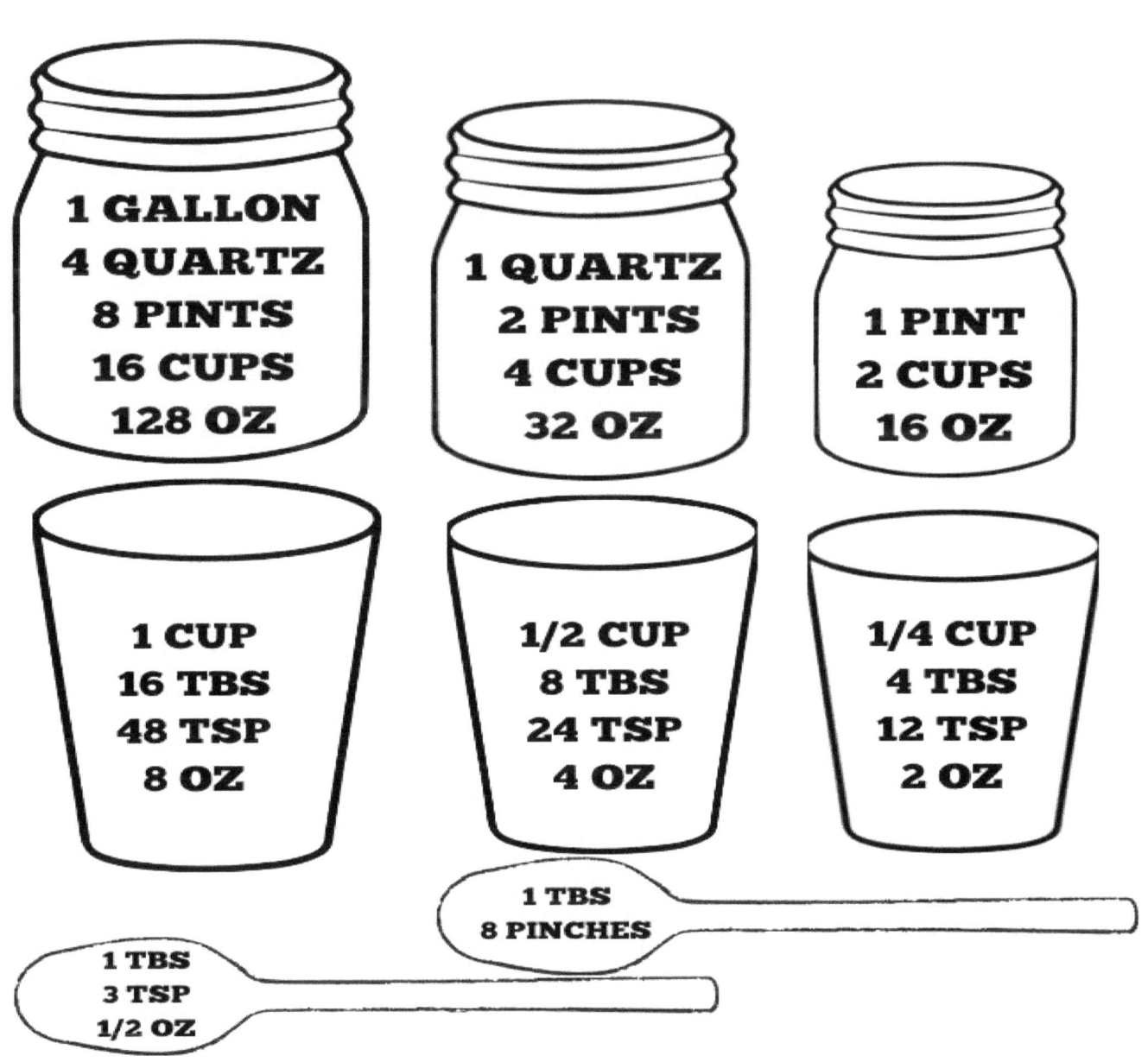

1 GALLON
4 QUARTZ
8 PINTS
16 CUPS
128 OZ

1 QUARTZ
2 PINTS
4 CUPS
32 OZ

1 PINT
2 CUPS
16 OZ

1 CUP
16 TBS
48 TSP
8 OZ

1/2 CUP
8 TBS
24 TSP
4 OZ

1/4 CUP
4 TBS
12 TSP
2 OZ

1 TBS
8 PINCHES

1 TBS
3 TSP
1/2 OZ

Dates

	BREAKFAST	LUNCH	DINNER	SNACKS
MON				
TUE				
WED				
THU				
FRI				
SAT				
SUN				

Shopping list

_____ _____ _____
_____ _____ _____
_____ _____ _____
_____ _____ _____
_____ _____ _____

Dates

	BREAKFAST	LUNCH	DINNER	SNACKS
MON				
TUE				
WED				
THU				
FRI				
SAT				
SUN				

Shopping list

Dates

	BREAKFAST	LUNCH	DINNER	SNACKS
MON				
TUE				
WED				
THU				
FRI				
SAT				
SUN				

Shopping list

_____   _____   _____
_____   _____   _____
_____   _____   _____
_____   _____   _____
_____   _____   _____
_____   _____   _____

Dates

	BREAKFAST	LUNCH	DINNER	SNACKS
MON				
TUE				
WED				
THU				
FRI				
SAT				
SUN				

Shopping list

GROCERY LIST

DATE: /   /

DAIRY:
- ○ _____
- ○ _____
- ○ _____
- ○ _____
- ○ _____
- ○ _____
- ○ _____
- ○ _____
- ○ _____
- ○ _____
- ○ _____
- ○ _____

MEAT & SEAFOOD:
- ○ _____
- ○ _____
- ○ _____
- ○ _____
- ○ _____
- ○ _____
- ○ _____
- ○ _____
- ○ _____
- ○ _____
- ○ _____
- ○ _____

FRUITS & VEGGIES:
- ○ _____
- ○ _____
- ○ _____
- ○ _____
- ○ _____
- ○ _____
- ○ _____
- ○ _____

BREAD & CEREAL:
- ○ _____
- ○ _____
- ○ _____
- ○ _____
- ○ _____

OTHERS:
- ○ _____
- ○ _____
- ○ _____
- ○ _____
- ○ _____
- ○ _____
- ○ _____

FROZEN FOODS:
- ○ _____
- ○ _____
- ○ _____
- ○ _____
- ○ _____

CANNED GOODS:
- ○ _____
- ○ _____
- ○ _____
- ○ _____
- ○ _____

WHAT'S COOKING:

S	
M	
T	
W	
T	
F	
S	

GROCERY LIST

DATE: /   /

DAIRY:
- ○ _____
- ○ _____
- ○ _____
- ○ _____
- ○ _____
- ○ _____
- ○ _____
- ○ _____
- ○ _____
- ○ _____
- ○ _____
- ○ _____

MEAT & SEAFOOD:
- ○ _____
- ○ _____
- ○ _____
- ○ _____
- ○ _____
- ○ _____
- ○ _____
- ○ _____
- ○ _____
- ○ _____
- ○ _____
- ○ _____

FRUITS & VEGGIES:
- ○ _____
- ○ _____
- ○ _____
- ○ _____
- ○ _____
- ○ _____
- ○ _____
- ○ _____

BREAD & CEREAL:
- ○ _____
- ○ _____
- ○ _____
- ○ _____
- ○ _____

OTHERS:
- ○ _____
- ○ _____
- ○ _____
- ○ _____
- ○ _____
- ○ _____
- ○ _____
- ○ _____
- ○ _____

FROZEN FOODS:
- ○ _____
- ○ _____
- ○ _____
- ○ _____
- ○ _____

CANNED GOODS:
- ○ _____
- ○ _____
- ○ _____
- ○ _____
- ○ _____

WHAT'S COOKING:
- S _____
- M _____
- T _____
- W _____
- T _____
- F _____
- S _____

Dear Reader,

Thank you for purchasing this cookbook. Creating this cookbook has been a labor of love, and I hope it has inspired you to explore new flavors and techniques in your kitchen. Each recipe has been crafted with care and passion, with the aim to cater to your health and diet requirements.

Your support means the world to me, and I am deeply grateful for your trust in my recipes. As you cook your way through the pages of this book, I hope you find as much joy in making these dishes as I did in creating them.

Jane Garraway

Your Feedback Matters

I would love to hear about your experiences with the recipes in this cookbook. Your honest reviews and feedback are incredibly valuable and help me continue to improve and share the joy of cooking with others. Whether it's a dish that turned out perfectly or one that you think could use some tweaking, your insights are welcomed and appreciated.

Please consider leaving a review on the platform where you purchased this book. Your feedback helps guide future books and ensures that I can continue to provide recipes that resonate with home cooks everywhere.

Thank you once again for your support.

www.ingramcontent.com/pod-product-compliance
Ingram Content Group UK Ltd.
Pitfield, Milton Keynes, MK11 3LW, UK
UKHW051436290925
8127UKWH00044B/1905